Disaster Risk Management in Agriculture

Disaster Risk Management in Agriculture

Case Studies in South Asian Countries

Edited by

Huong Ha
School of Business
Singapore University of Social Sciences
Singapore

R. Lalitha S. Fernando
Department of Public Administration
University of Sri Jayewardenepura
Nugegoda, Sri Lanka

Sanjeev Kumar Mahajan
Himachal Pradesh University
Shimla, India

BEP BUSINESS EXPERT PRESS

Disaster Risk Management in Agriculture: Case Studies in South Asian Countries
Copyright © Business Expert Press, LLC, 2019.

First published in 2019 by
Business Expert Press, LLC
222 East 46th Street, New York, NY 10017
www.businessexpertpress.com

ISBN-13: 978-1-94944-315-8 (paperback)
ISBN-13: 978-1-94944-316-5 (e-book)

Business Expert Press Economics and Public Policy Collection

Collection ISSN: 2163-761X (print)
Collection ISSN: 2163-7628 (electronic)

Cover and interior design by S4Carlisle Publishing Services Private Ltd., Chennai, India

First edition: 2019

10 9 8 7 6 5 4 3 2 1

Printed in the United States of America.

Abstract

The issues and challenges related to disaster risk management (DRM) in the agricultural sector are now widely linked to sustainable environment. The fact remains that almost every day a disaster strikes some part of the world. The regular occurrence of disasters, both natural and man-made, has forced the worldwide communities to look for novel solutions to prevent and mitigate such disasters. It has also compelled the attention of academicians and practitioners to seek solutions using DRM strategies in the context of the agricultural sector. This volume compiles probing studies that disseminate the work of outstanding scholars and practitioners, especially in South Asian countries. The research studies focus on how to tackle the challenges associated with disasters at the ground level. Thus emerges the need to amalgamate and coordinate the resources and agencies involved in DRM in agriculture to ensure the quality of life to the citizens of the affected countries after disasters.

This volume incorporates specific themes correlated with DRM from the perspective of South Asia. It assesses (i) the consequences of distinct disaster risks in agriculture, (ii) how diverse disaster risk problems are handled in distinct settings, and (iii) different methodologies embraced by different sectors of society to alleviate and prepare for disaster risk. This volume adopts an interdisciplinary approach to examine various aspects of disaster risk management with regard to governance, including policy making, implementation, and monitoring.

Keywords

disaster risk management (DRM); agriculture; South Asia; multidisciplinary approach; stakeholders; sustainable environment

Contents

List of Figures

List of Tables

List of Reviewers

Prof. Namrata Agrawal (National Institute of Financial Management, India)

Mr. Md Zahir Ahmed (Policy Research Centre bd, Bangladesh)

Dr. Misa Aoki (Nara Women's University, Japan)

Senior Prof. R. Lalitha S. Fernando (University of Sri Jayewardenepura, Nugegoda, Sri Lanka)

Dr. Huong Ha (Singapore University of Social Sciences, Singapore).

Ms. Nahian Nabila Hoque (Legal Council in Bangladesh)

Dr. Shafiq Islam (CRP, Savar, Dhaka, Bangladesh)

Dr. Jak Jabes (Independent Researcher, Canada)

Prof. Dr. Neena Joseph (Independent Researcher, India)

Prof. Kalpana Kharad (K.J. Somaiya College of Education, India)

Prof. Dr. Sarfraz Khawaja (Civil Services Academy, Lahore, Pakistan)

Prof. Dr. Steven Leibo (Russell Sage College, USA)

Prof. Dr. Sanjeev Kumar Mahajan (Himachal Pradesh University, India)

Mr. Himanshu Shekhar Mishra (New Delhi Television, India)

A/Prof. Md Nurul Momen (University of Rajshahi, Bangladesh)

A/Prof. Dr. Isaias S. Sealza (Xavier University, Philippines)

Dr. Olivia Tan Swee Leng (Multimedia University, Malaysia)

Dr. Stanley Bruce Thomson (Federation Business School at Federation University, Australia)

Acknowledgments

The editors take pride in acknowledging the role of the *Network of Asia-Pacific Schools and Institutes of Public Administration and Governance* popularly known by the acronym NAPSIPAG in making the present book possible. NAPSIPAG is the largest governance research network in the Asia-Pacific region that has been regularly organizing an international meeting of administrators, academia, and nonstate bodies every year where regional scholars critically deliberate with international governance experts. This is the process through which many young and upcoming scholars are also trained and academic brilliance generated. NAPSIPAG has also helped the international policy organizations to have a better understanding about the region through the local lens of Asiatic anthropology, ethnography, and culture of administration. The book is an outcome of the academic and practitioners' discourses generated mainly by NAPSIPAG members.

It was impossible for this book to be completed without the support of members, the reviewers, the authors, family members, and friends. The editors take pride in acknowledging the great role of the reviewers and the authors. The editor wishes to thank (i) the reviewers for their professional and constructive feedback that is valuable to the authors, (ii) the contributing authors for their cooperation during the revision stages, and (iii) Dr. Stanley Bruce Thomson for his exceptional and tireless support during the review and proofreading processes. Finally, the editors are very grateful for the advice and assistance from the series editor/s of BEP, USA.

Dr. Huong Ha
Prof. R. Lalitha S. Fernando
Prof. Sanjeev Kumar Mahajan

CHAPTER 1

Disaster Risk Management in Agriculture: Case Studies in South Asia—An Introduction

Huong Ha

School of Business, Singapore University of Social Sciences, Singapore

Sanjeev Kumar Mahajan

Himachal Pradesh University, Shimla, India

R. Lalitha S. Fernando

Department of Public Administration, University of Sri Jayewardenepura, Sri Lanka

Introduction

Disasters entail serious consequences to all groups of stakeholders, including the environment, at all levels, international, regional, national, and local. To the agricultural sector, disasters are synonymous with loss of crops and productivity, loss of livelihood among farmers and those who work in supporting sectors, soil degradation, and many other damages. To countries that rely heavily on agriculture, especially South Asian countries, disasters in agriculture hinder socioeconomic development and erode the effort to eliminate hunger and alleviate poverty. Since disasters cannot be avoided or negotiated, whether in agriculture or any other sector, disaster risk management (DRM) should be prioritized in the government's agenda for national economic development and should receive the urgent attention of all groups of stakeholders.

The PreventionWeb (n.d.) discusses four categories of natural hazard-induced disasters—"(i) drought and other meteorological and climatological disasters, (ii) floods, (iii) geophysical-related disasters, such as earthquakes and tsunamis, and (iv) 'biological disasters (epidemics, infestations, and animal disease)'" (para. 3). All these disasters affect the agriculture sector and its subsectors in one or many ways. The updated statistics pertaining to natural disasters affecting the agriculture sector in South Asia show a rise in the number of casualties and physical damage. In the South Asian region, the number of natural disasters in 2016 was 342 (Guha-Sapir et al. 2016). Internal displacements in India, Nepal, Sri Lanka, and Pakistan totaled 1,346,000, 384,000, 135,000, and 1,800, respectively (*The Jakarta Post* 2018).

According to the Food and Agriculture Organization of the United Nations (FAO 2015), natural disasters affected more than 1.9 billion people and entailed an estimated damage of $494 billion in developing countries. From the FAO's assessment of 78 disasters, the damage in the agricultural sector and subsectors was $93 billion during the period 2005 to 2014 (Food and Agriculture Organization of the United Nations 2017). Generally, the agricultural sector absorbs approximately 23 percent of the economic losses caused by natural hazards and disasters in developing countries in 2014 (Food and Agriculture Organization of the United Nations 2008, 2017, 2018b).

Given social, physical, and human capital resources constraints, this raises the following questions: "Can disasters be better managed in South Asia? And how can risk pertaining to the agricultural sector be better mitigated?" This volume attempts to present academic and practical work with regard to DRM in agriculture in different contexts in South Asian countries. The main objectives of this volume are to analyze (i) the impact of different types of disaster risks on agriculture; (ii) how different disaster risk and related issues in the agricultural sector have been managed; and

(iii) different approaches adopted by countries to plan, manage, and prepare for disaster risk in the context of the agricultural sector in South Asia.

The eight chapters, excluding the introduction and the conclusion, included in this book were written by industry practitioners and academia from various South Asian countries. This has enhanced the breadth and significance of the discussion. The distinctiveness of this volume is the inclusion of special topics such as the health of women; food security; data analytics; and disasters, nuclear disasters, and floods; and sustainable development, which have rarely been treated elaborately in the literature.

Issues and Challenges Associated with Disaster Risk in Agriculture in South Asia

It is an undisputable fact that South Asia is perpetually hit by natural disasters, and, consequently, the development process in some countries has been impeded. This has led to environmental degradation, affecting the lives of the people and their livelihoods. Exposure to losses resulting from natural disasters is increasing worldwide, affecting livelihoods and food security. There are currently 842 million undernourished people around the world (Food and Agriculture Organization of the United Nations 2018a).

The United Nations' 2030 Agenda for Sustainable Development, laid down for its 193 member nations, states that they should prepare themselves to effectively prevent and mitigate the impact of the disasters. Agriculture needs focused attention and should be at the center stage of any nation. It is evident that climate and agriculture are closely linked, as climate is a primary factor in agricultural production. Because of the high level of carbon dioxide, future projections of climate change indicate increasing temperature and varied rainfall, both of which will greatly impact the agricultural sector (Srivalsan et al. 2017). This will lead to more natural disasters and negative impacts on agriculture and the natural environment. Disasters entail negative effects on agricultural output, in the short and long term, and hence affect economic growth (Cavello et al. 2010).

Disaster risk reduction measures are necessary to reduce, prevent, and mitigate the consequences and impact of disasters on the agricultural sector (Ha 2014, 2017; Ha, Fernando and Mahmood 2015a, b). Agricultural growth and productivity depend on food production systems that are resilient against production failures arising from shocks and climate variability. This requires strong emphasis or sector-specific disaster risk reduction measures, technologies, and practices as well as sustainable use and management of vital resources, such as land, water, soil nutrients, and genetic resources (Food and Agriculture Organization of the United Nations 2015).

An Overview of the Chapters

The first chapter (Chapter 2), by Namrata Agrawal and Disha Gupta, employs a multidimensional approach to the analysis of the adverse effects of natural disasters on agriculture, using data analytics (Detwiler 2016). The chapter analyzes the trends in damage or loss to lives, crops, cattle, and property over the last thirteen years in India. The authors also explore the correlations between variables and discuss how such damages and losses by natural disasters affect the livelihood of the victims and India's economy, in general. The findings suggest that there is a direct relationship between (i) the number of damaged houses and the number of lives lost and vice versa and (ii) the number of lives lost and the crop areas affected. The authors propose that stakeholders should invest more in research and development (R&D) in terms of disaster preparedness, mitigation, and prevention and that adequate funds should be available for such R&D projects.

In Chapter 3, Rajesh Kumar refers to the nuclear disaster in Fukushima in 2011 that damaged several farmhouses and fishing trawlers and resulted in radioactive contamination of soil, crops, and marine areas (Farrell 2018; Morino, Nishizawa, and Ohara 2011). The debate on nuclear power has been ongoing and intensive. On the one hand, the world relies on nuclear power for future consumption, while on the other hand, there are no established safeguards to ensure that mega nuclear power projects remain free from nuclear disasters. Thus, this chapter discusses how India should prepare for nuclear disasters and how it can become a disaster-resilient country. The author also conducted a primary survey of 350 university students in Amritsar district of Indian Punjab to assess the level of participants' awareness of nuclear disasters. The findings suggest that their level of awareness was very low. Thus, there is a need to improve the dissemination of relevant information to different groups of stakeholders, especially young people, in order to build a culture of nuclear disaster resilience in India (Government of India Planning Commission 2011). Education on disaster preparation and mitigation should start from the beginning, that is, at an early age, so that young people will acquire a good understanding of the causes and effects of disasters and cultivate good habits for DRM (Abhas and Stanton-Geddes 2013).

In Chapter 4, Lalitha Fernando, Dimuthu Kumari, and Dissanayaka discuss various approaches to building a resilient society to prepare for and manage natural disasters in Sri Lanka. They also discuss good practices for sustainable agriculture. The authors observe that the existing agricultural policy in Sri Lanka has been developed, reviewed, and revised intensively and covers a wide range of issues but that its implementation is not strictly enforced. This chapter aims to (i) analyze the strengths and weaknesses of the existing agricultural policies in Sri Lanka, (ii) identify issues associated with the implementation of such policies, and (iii) make policy recommendations with regard to good practices to manage disasters. Such practices include the need to improve public awareness of disaster-related risk, provide support to farmers to build a culture of resilient agriculture, introduce and familiarize farmers with livelihood diversification practices and the use of organic fertilizers, and facilitate the process to obtain credit and access safety nets. The authors concur with the Federal Ministry of Agriculture & Rural Development in Nigeria (2016) that coordination among agricultural institutions should be strengthened.

In Chapter 5, Nasim Banu categorizes different types of natural disasters that affect agricultural production in Bangladesh (Del Nfnno et al. 2001; George 2017). Government agencies have taken initiatives and introduced programs to mitigate damages and losses caused by natural disasters and environmental stress to the agricultural sector. This chapter aims to identify the common natural disasters that impede the growth of agricultural output in Bangladesh and to assess the plans and programs in place to protect agricultural losses and damages from natural disasters in order to ensure food security and environmental sustainability in the country. According to the author, the Government of Bangladesh has undertaken various initiatives to mitigate disaster risk and to protect mainstream agricultural output from natural calamities and climate change issues by midterm and long-term planning and budgetary considerations (a subject that has also been discussed by Rawlani and Sovacool (2011)). The author makes a number of recommendations, namely:

I. disseminating the information about disasters and disaster forecasting by issuing weather bulletins and warning signals,

II. implementing public education and community mobilization activities to enhance public awareness with regard to preparation and response to disasters,

III. introducing proper mechanisms to protect the coastal areas and river banks to minimize inundation and reduce the harmfulness of saline, and

IV. effective land and forestation management, engaging local communities. These are consistent with what has been discussed by Ha, Fernando, and Mahmood (2015a, b) and Rogers and Tsirkunov (2010).

In Chapter 6, Sanjeev Kumar Mahajan and Anupama Puri Mahajan focus on two key issues, namely, hazards and the vulnerability profile of Himachal Pradesh in India, and the damages resulting from heavy rainfall. In addition, earthquakes are some of the biggest threats in this state because of its geographical position (Government of Himachal Pradesh 2012). In terms of vulnerability profile, Himachal Pradesh state has four agroecological zones, and water shortage or excess rainfall has occurred. The authors observe that disasters have affected the agricultural sector in many ways and call for risk reduction and management to be "systematically embedded into the agricultural sector" (Chapter 6), as discussed by the Food and Agriculture Organization of the United Nations (2008), and Baas, Ramasamy, DePryck and Battista (2008).

Chapter 7, by Rabindranath Bhattacharyya and Jebunnessa, focuses on a very important issue, namely, that the agricultural sector needs to achieve food security. This chapter compares and contrasts the public (food) distribution systems in postdisaster situations in Bangladesh and West Bengal (India). The authors observe that West Bengal and Bangladesh share certain similarities such as topography, ecosystems, environmental hazards, language, and cultural and historical heritage, and that it is therefore justifiable to compare and contrast the similarities and differences between the public (food) distribution systems in these two jurisdictions. Bangladesh has a Public Food Distribution System (PFDS), and West Bengal has a similar system, called Targeted Public Distribution System (TPDS) (Islam 2014; World Food Programme 2014). However, the outcomes of these two systems may not be the same, especially in postdisaster situations. Thus, the chapter aims to examine (i) the extent to which these two systems can reach the recipients in these two areas, (ii) the capacity of these systems to ensure food security after disasters, and (iii) the factors that influence the effectiveness of these systems. It was found that the public food distribution systems in Bangladesh and West Bengal have shifted from food grain distribution through fair price ration shops in order to distribute food to vulnerable groups (Muniruzzaman 2013). In West Bengal, a strong TPDS network and the insurance coverage of the loss of crops caused by disasters have been instrumental in ensuring food security for the populace (Bhattacharyya 2018), unlike in Bangladesh, where the insurance coverage for the loss of crops caused by disasters is not substantial, driving the recipients to depend heavily on the PFDS during crises (Ozaki 2016).

The last chapter, by Himanshu Shekhar Mishra, discusses how floods affect sustainable development, using Srinagar and Chennai as a case study. The impact of Chennai's devastating floods on the critical infrastructure of the province is examined. The study highlights the severe and adverse effects of the floods on the victims in the affected areas and the destruction of public and private properties and assets worth billions of dollars (Shannon et al. 2013). The study uncovers "the fault lines in India's disaster management strategy and expose[s] the weaknesses in its disaster relief and response mechanism" (Chapter 8). Concurring with the position taken by the UNISDR (2014), the chapter explains that there is an urgent need to incorporate disaster risk reduction measures in the context of the agricultural sector in the disaster governance framework of India.

Lessons: Rebuilding Agriculture after Disaster

Sustainable development results in finding different approaches to achieving socioeconomic and environmental goals, keeping in view the capacities of the government and without sacrificing the interests of individuals for the sake of others. DRM and sustainability are the key to achieving sustainable development goals by 2030 (UNISDR n.d.).

Changes in weather and climate across the globe, especially in South Asia, have challenged all the nations to reassess their DRM systems. The thrust is on addressing short-term climate variations and ensuring that different sectors and systems should become resilient and adaptable to the changing risks over the long term.

Rebuilding disaster-struck areas is an enormous task in any country at the regional and local levels. It is also evident that although agriculture is the main source of livelihood in many South Asian countries, it has become risky because of the impact of climate change (OECD 2015). However, to protect the community, it is essential that steps be taken to reduce the adverse effects of disasters on agriculture.

Disaster risk reduction and management policies need to be drafted carefully, and each country must understand the topography and conditions minutely. Policy makers should adopt a regional focus rather than relying on models relevant to the needs of other countries. These considerations call for the following strategies:

- Access to localized warning systems to help the local farming community in decision making.
- Crop insurance in disaster-prone areas should be made compulsory (World Bank 2005) as this measure can provide strong social protection.
- Increased financial investment should be high on the agenda of the Government. To generate more resources for research in agriculture, an effort should be made to rope in the private sector.

Finally, a rigorous sense of caution should guard against any tendency to play with nature. Countries should adopt a special focus on maintaining and preserving their water bodies to avoid clogging and allow the free movement of water through their natural channels. It is high time that man learned to live with nature rather than to exploit it.

Conclusion

This chapter has discussed the issues and challenges facing DRM in the context of the agricultural sector. Although governments and different political sectors in South Asian countries have made an effort to prepare for and mitigate disaster risk, several factors such as governance, leadership, resources, mechanisms, and institutions hinder their efforts and shape the outcomes, making the disaster risk process more challenging, especially in the agricultural sector.

One of the conclusions reached by this book is that there is a chain effect operating among issues and between issues and solutions. For example, natural disasters cause damages and losses in crops and livestock, reducing agricultural production. The reduction in agricultural output, in turn, affects food security. Thus, policy makers and legislators should be well acquainted with agriculture-related issues associated with disasters in order to create feasible and effective laws and policies. Furthermore, as good policies do not produce desirable outcomes unless effectively implemented, strong enforcement mechanisms should be in place. Second, DRM is not a task performed solo by a single stakeholder or group of stakeholders. Rather, it is the collective effort of all groups of stakeholders in every sector. Finally, there is a strong interdependence among activities and between policies and implementation to address the issues associated with DRM in the agricultural sector. A strong culture of resilience would contribute to the mitigation of disaster risk in the agricultural sector and its subsectors.

References

Abhas, K.J., and Z. Stanton-Geddes, eds. 2013. *Strong, Safe, and Resilient: A Strategic Policy Guide for Disaster Risk Management in East Asia and the Pacific*. Washington, DC: World Bank.

Baas, S., S. Ramasamy, J.D. DePryck, and F. Battista. 2008. *Disaster Risk Management Systems Analysis*. Rome, France: The Food and Agriculture Organization of the United Nations.

Bhattacharyya, R. 2018. "Can Laws Ensure Disaster Risk Reduction? A Study of Mandarmani Sea Beach in West Bengal." In *Disaster Law Emerging Thresholds*, ed. A. Singh, (pp. 345–358). New York, NY: Routledge.

Cavalla, E., S. Galiani, O. Noy, and J. Pantano. 2010. *Catastrophic Natural Disasters and Economic Growth.* https://pdfs.semanticscholar.org/5dc5/dbf79095fa14565e0807916dc2092a1233c6.pdf

Del Nfnno, C., P.A. Dorosh, L.C. Smith, and D.K. Roy. 2001. *The 1998 Floods in Bangladesh: Disaster, Impacts, Household Coping Strategies, and Response.* Research Report 122. Washington, DC: International Food Policy Research Institute.

Detwiler, J. 2016. *Geospatial Big Data Analytics.* University Park, PA: Penn State, College of Earth & Mineral Sciences.

Farrell, J. 2018. "Fukushima Nuclear Disaster: Lethal Levels of Radiation Detected in Leak Seven Years After Plant Meltdown in Japan." *The Independent.* www.independent.co.uk

Federal Ministry of Agriculture & Rural Development, Nigeria. 2016. *The Agriculture Promotion Policy (2016–2020): Building on the Successes of the ATA, Closing Key Gaps.* Abuja FCT: Federal Ministry of Agriculture & Rural Development, Nigeria.

Food and Agriculture Organization of the United Nations. 2008. *Good Practices for Hazard Risk Management in Agriculture: Summary Report Jamaica.* Rome, France: Food and Agriculture Organization of the United Nations.

Food and Agriculture Organization of the United Nations. 2015. *The Impact of Natural Hazards and Disasters on Agriculture and Food Security and Nutrition: A Call for Action to Build Resilient Livelihoods.* Rome, France: Food and Agriculture Organization of the United Nations.

Food and Agriculture Organization of the United Nations. 2017. *The Impact of Disasters on Agriculture Addressing the Information Gap.* Rome, France: Food and Agriculture Organization of the United Nations. http://www.fao.org/3/a-i7279e.pdf

Food and Agriculture Organization of the United Nations. 2018a. *The State of Food Security and Nutrition around the World.* Rome, France: Food and Agriculture Organization of the United Nations.

Food and Agriculture Organization of the United Nations. 2018b. *2017 The Impact of Disasters and Crises on Agriculture and Food Security.* Rome, France: Food and Agriculture Organization of the United Nations.

George, S. 2017. A Third of Bangladesh Under Water as Flood Devastation Widens. *CNN* (Cable News Network), September 1, 2017.

https://edition.cnn.com/2017/09/01/asia/bangladesh-south-asia-floods/index.html

Government of Himachal Pradesh. 2012. *Himachal Pradesh State Disaster Management Plan.* Disaster Management Cell. Shimla: Revenue Department.

Government of India Planning Commission. 2011. *Disaster Management for the Twelfth Five Year Plan* (2012-2017). India: Government of India Planning Commission.

Guha-Sapir, D., P. Hoyois, P. Wallemacq, and R. Below. 2016. "Annual Disaster Statistical Review 2016: The Numbers and Trends." https://reliefweb.int/report/world/annual-disaster-statistical-review-2016-numbers-and-trends

Ha, H. 2014. "Land Use and Disaster Governance in Asia: An Introduction." In *Land and Disaster Management Strategies in Asia*, ed. H. Ha, (pp. 1–14). Germany/New Delhi: Springer.

Ha, H. 2017. "Risk Governance and Disaster Impacts in Asia." PreventionWeb, UN Office for Disaster Risk Reduction. http://www.preventionweb.net/experts/oped/view/55397

Ha, H., L. Fernando, and A. Mahmood. 2015a. "Disaster Management in Asia: Lessons Learned and Policy Implications." In *Strategic Disaster Risk Management in Asia*, eds. H. Ha, L. Fernando, and A. Mahmood, (pp. 221–6). Germany/New Delhi: Springer.

Ha, H., L. Fernando, and A. Mahmood. 2015b. "Strategic Disaster Risk Management in Asia: An Introduction." In *Strategic Disaster Risk Management in Asia*, eds. H. Ha, L. Fernando, and A. Mahmood, (pp. 1–13). Germany/New Delhi: Springer.

Islam, M.M. 2014. "The Politics of the Public Food Distribution System in Bangladesh: Regime Survival or Promoting Food Security?" *Journal of Asian and African Studies* 50, no. 6, pp. 702–15.

Morino, Y., M. Nishizawa, and T. Ohara. 2011. "Atmospheric Behavior Deposition, and Budget of Radioactive Materials from the Fukushima Daiichi Nuclear Power Plant in March 2011." *Geophysical Research Letters* 38, p. L00GII. doi:10.1029/2011GL048689, 2011.

Muniruzzaman, A.N.M. 2013. "Food Security in Bangladesh: A Comprehensive Analysis." *Peace and Security Review* 5, no. 10, pp. 46–73.

Organisation for Economic Co-operation and Development. 2015. *Agriculture and Climate Change*. Paris: OECD.

Ozaki, M. 2016. "Disaster Risk Financing in Bangladesh, ADB South Asia." Working Paper Series, No. 46. Manila: Asian Development Bank.

PreventionWeb. n.d. *The Impact of Disasters on Agriculture: Addressing the Information Gap.* PreventionWeb.

Rawlani, A.K., and B.K. Sovacool. 2011. "Building Responsiveness to Climate Change through Community Based Adaptation in Bangladesh." *Mitigation and Adaptation Strategies for Global Change* 16, no. 8, pp. 845–63.

Rogers, D., and V. Tsirkunov. 2010. *Implementing Hazard Early Warning Systems: GFDRR WCIDS Report 11-03.* PreventionWeb.

Shannon, D., A. Daniels, S. Murray, and T. D. Kirsch. 2013. "The Human Impact of Floods: A Historical Review of Events 1980-2009 and Systematic Literature Review." *PLOS Currents Disasters* 2013 Apr 16, Edition 1, pp. 1–34. doi:10.1371/currents.dis.f4deb457904936b 07c09daa98ee8171a.

Srivalsan, V., J. Hur, J. Liu, N.S. Nguyen, Y. Sun, and S.-Y. Liong. 2017. *Distributional impacts of climate change and food security in Southeast Asia.* ERIA. http://www.eria.org/ERIA-DP-2016-41.pdf

The Jakarta Post. 2018. "Internal Displacement in Asia Due to Natural Disasters." *The Jakarta Post,* 25 July 2018. http://www.thejakartapost.com/news/2018/07/25/internal-displacement-in-asia-due-to-natural-disasters.html

United Nations Office for Disaster Risk Reduction. 2014. "Contribution to the 2014 United Nations Economic and Social Council (ECOSOC) Integration Segment." http://www.un.org/en/ecosoc/integration/pdf/unisdr.pdf

United Nations Office for Disaster Risk Reduction. n.d. *UNISDR Strategic Framework 2016-2021.* Geneva, Switzerland: UNISDR.

World Bank. 2005. *Managing Agricultural Production Risks: Innovations in Developing Countries.* World Bank Agriculture and Rural Development Department, Report No. 32727. Washington, DC: World Bank.

World Food Programme. 2014. *Targeted Public Distribution System Best Practice Solution.* New Delhi: World Food Programme.

CHAPTER 2

Pragmatic Study of the Impact of Disasters on Humans and Agriculture Using Data Analytics

Namrata Agrawal

NIFM, *Ministry of Finance, Government of India, India*

Disha Gupta

Gujarat Forensic Sciences University, Gandhinagar, Gujarat, India

Introduction

India has regularly faced natural disasters because of its unique geo-climatic conditions. This chapter highlights the existing disaster vulnerability in India. Around 57 percent of land in India is vulnerable to earthquakes, of which 12 percent is vulnerable to severe earthquakes, 12 percent to floods, and 8 percent to cyclones. The number of climate-induced disasters has increased significantly over the last decade. Of all the natural hazards, floods, droughts, and tropical storms affect the agricultural sector, most depicting the severe impact of climate-related disasters. Apart from natural disasters, some cities in India are also vulnerable to chemical and industrial disasters and other man-made disasters (NPDM 2009).

Since 1950, there has been a gradual increase in the economic costs linked with all natural disasters. After each decade, there has been a rising trend in the number of deaths due to natural disasters (around 50 percent), as compared with the population growth rate of around 20 percent. World-wide, annual economic costs related to natural disasters have been estimated at $50 to $100 billion (FAO 2015). It is predicted that by the year 2050, 100,000 lives will be lost globally each year because of natural disasters and that the global cost could be $300 billion annually (CRED 2017).

This chapter adopts a multidimensional approach through an empirical study and analysis of the impact of natural disasters on humans and agriculture by exhaustive analysis of the data on natural disasters in India during the period 2001 to 2013. The data/figures and statistics have been collected from various ministries of the government of India for the study.

The chapter also highlights the yearwise trend analysis of disasters and the probable reasons thereof, including the analysis of the correlations between various vital parameters such as lives lost, cropped areas affected, and cattle lost.

Research Objectives

The objective of the study was to understand and analyze the trends in natural disasters occurring in India over the last thirteen years. Modern analytical tools and techniques have been used to study the correlations between the vital parameters such as "lives lost" (in numbers), "cattle lost" (in numbers), "houses damaged" (in numbers), and "cropped areas affected" (in million ha) with respect to the natural disasters that took place. The research findings/outcomes will be shared with the stakeholders/Government/decision makers for informed and effective decision making in the future.

Methodology

The data set comprises annual loss figures that occurred because of natural disasters from 2001 to 2013 in India. The data set was obtained from various ministries such as Indian Meteorological Department, Ministry of Health and Family Welfare, Ministry of Agriculture and Animal Husbandry, Ministry of Environment and Forests, and Ministry of Labour. The data set was collated to focus on the statistics on annual lives lost, cattle lost, houses damaged, and cropped areas affected from 2001 until 2013.

Data analytics tools, such as Tableau, Statpro, and Excel, were used to analyze the impact of natural disasters on agriculture, human lives, cattle lost, and houses damaged in the last thirteen years in India with a critical perspective (Evans 2016).

The following analysis was performed on the collated data set:

A) Trend analysis to reflect the trends in damage/loss to lives in the last thirteen years arising from natural disasters in India;
B) Trend analysis to find the trends related to damage of cropped areas in the last thirteen years;
C) To study and analyze the relationships/correlations between various parameters listed here for improved decision making in future:
   C.1 Relationship between lives lost and houses damaged
   C.2 Relationship between lives lost and cattle lost
   C.3 Relationship between lives lost and cropped areas affected
D) Assessment of the wider impact of natural disasters on the value chain on agro-industries, national economics, livelihoods, and food security in India.

The findings were graphically depicted to facilitate understanding, decision making, and drawing of conclusions.

Findings

The observations and results obtained from the analysis of the data have been elaborated as follows:

Trend analysis of loss of lives on account of disasters in the last thirteen years in India

- In Figure 2.1, the rise in the number of lives lost during 2001–2002 may be attributed to the massive earthquake that occurred on January 26, 2001, in Kutch district of the state of Gujarat, which killed around 20,000 people.

- The heat wave in the southern part of India that killed more than 1,000 people in the state of Andhra Pradesh is a probable reason for the rise in the number of causalities during the years 2002–2003 (Figure 2.1).

- The rise in the graph during the year 2003–2004 reflects the rise in casualties because of the Indian Ocean earthquake/tsunami that occurred on the west coast of Sumatra. However, during the year 2004–2005, there was no significant loss of lives, resulting in a horizontal line in Figure 2.1.

- The steep rise in the loss of human lives between the years 2006 and 2007 is a consequence of floods in Bihar, a flood-prone state in India. This was the worst disaster in Bihar in the last 30 years.

- There is a steep fall in the number of lives lost between the years 2008–2009 and 2009–2010 because of comparatively fewer or insignificant natural calamities in the entire country.

- The graph rises slightly between the years 2010 and 2011 presumably because of the eastern Indian storm that killed more than 90 people and destroyed or damaged around 91,000 dwellings.

- There were comparatively less cases of natural disasters during the years 2011–2012 (till May 2013) as reflected in the graph below.

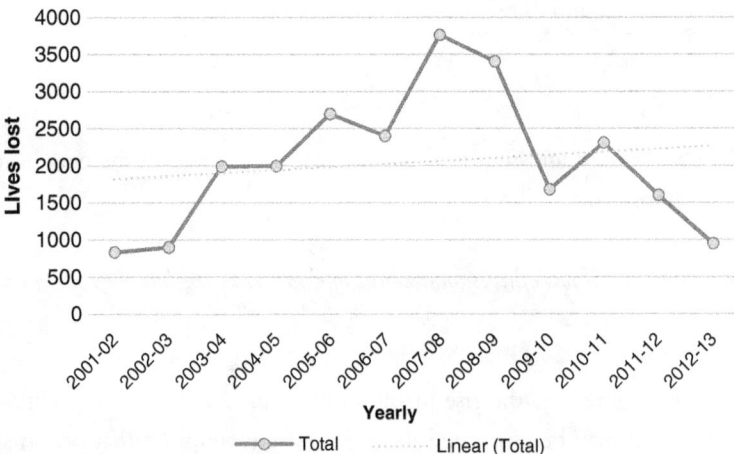

Figure 2.1 Yearwise lives lost (in numbers)

Trend analysis of cropped areas affected by disasters in the last thirteen years in India

- Figure 2.2 shows that there was relatively less damage to crops from 2001 up to 2006, as natural calamities, if any, generally affected human beings.
- The maximum loss of cropped areas occurred between the years 2005–2006 and 2007–2008 and may be attributed to the Bihar floods and the deficient monsoon in the country as a whole.
- The trend was relatively constant between the years 2009–2010 and 2010–2011 but declined in subsequent years.

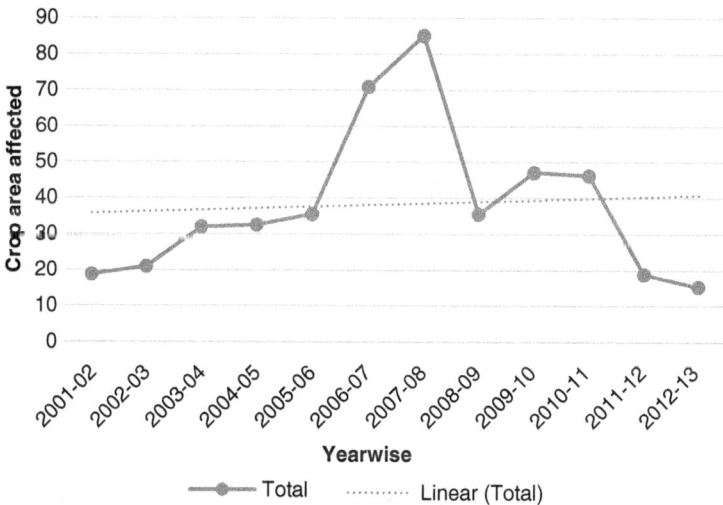

Figure 2.2 Yearwise crop area affected

Relationships/Correlations between Vital Parameters

Relationship between Lives Lost and Cropped Areas Affected

Every natural disaster adversely affects the human resources of a nation, resulting in demotivated homeless survivors. The livelihoods of the affected populace were impacted to the extent that they depend solely on the relief measures of the government.

The correlation between the lives lost and the cropped areas affected has been calculated to determine the relationship (if any) that exists between them.

- It is evident from Figure 2.3 that there is a positive correlation of 0.735 between the number of lives lost and the extent of cropped areas affected. This implies that a rise in human casualty figures would eventually indicate a rise in the adversely affected cropped areas.
- This analysis is accurate and practical, as more damages to human resources would have a larger bearing on agricultural damage. Ultimately, it is human beings who take care of the cropped areas.

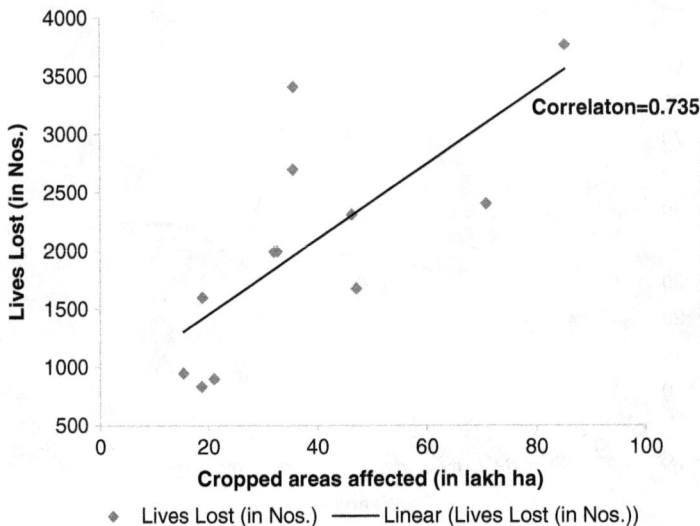

Figure 2.3 Correlation between lives lost and cropped areas affected

Relationship between Lives Lost and Houses Damaged

- Data analysis of the natural disaster figures for the period 2001 to 2013 and subsequent study of the relationship between the number of lives lost and houses damaged has been performed (Figure 2.4).
- A strong positive correlation of 0.873 between the parameters number of lives lost and houses damaged indicates that any increase in the number of damaged houses has eventually resulted in an increased number of lives lost and vice versa. This holds practically true and factual.

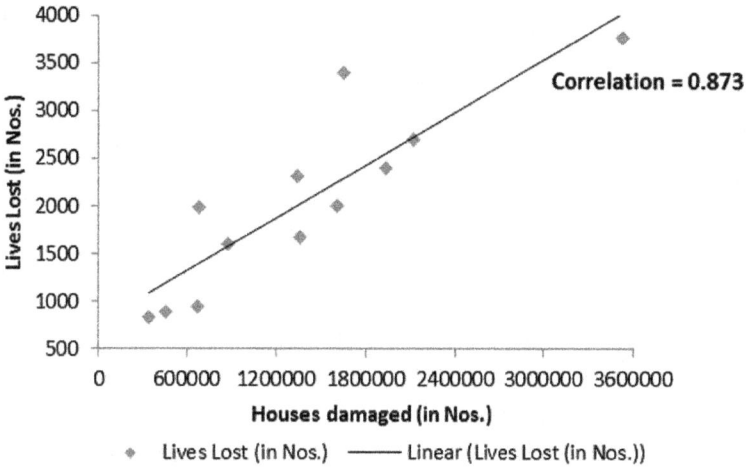

Figure 2.4 *Correlation between lives lost and houses damaged*

Relationship between Lives Lost and Cattle Lost

- It is observed that there is a relatively weak correlation, 0.322, between the number of lives lost and number of cattle lost, indicating that an increase in cattle loss would not eventually lead to an increase in lives lost and vice versa (Figure 2.5). However, this is indicative of the positive rising trends.

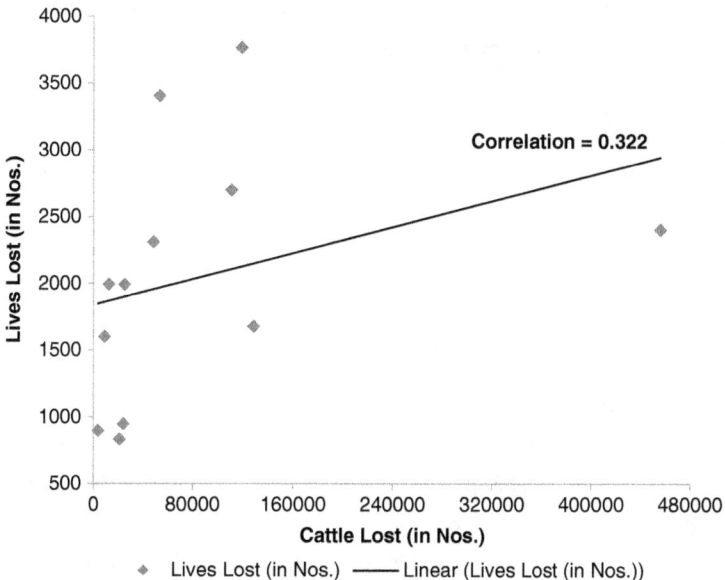

Figure 2.5 *Correlation between lives lost and cattle lost*

The above findings and trends constitute a strong warning to all (major/minor) stakeholders concerned to collaborate and work together to minimize redundancy of the efforts and to evolve systematic and effective information reporting and monitoring tools for preparedness, immediate response, and damage assessment.

Conclusion

The findings of the study generally exhibit a rising trend of adversities. The study suggests that the potential of information technology may be exploited to check the rising trend of natural disasters. Further, the National Policy on Disaster Management of India should be revisited for a holistic and practical approach to the implementation of prevention, mitigation, and preparedness in the predisaster phase with appropriate additional funding, along with the extant policy on postdisaster relief and rehabilitation under crisis management.

As the number of natural disasters is on the rise and continues to significantly impact the world's poorest and least-developed countries, emphasis must be placed on appropriate and informed investment toward disaster reduction.

It is necessary to include as a key component R&D work in disaster preparedness, mitigation, and prevention so that adequate funds are earmarked for the schemes of R&D organizations as well as the central ministries and state governments concerned.

Recommendations

The broad assessment of the impact of natural disasters on agriculture, housing, and human lives points to the urgent need for a holistic integrated approach toward safeguarding them. Programs for improving methods of prediction and dissemination of warnings should be expanded and intensified. Stakeholders' efforts are also needed to determine the impact of disasters on natural resources. Priority should be given to research with practical applications leading to an understanding of physical and biological factors contributing to disasters.

Further, effective and practical guidelines need to be issued to ministries or departments concerned of the Government of India to integrate the measures for prevention of disasters or their mitigation in development plans and projects.

The potential of information technology can be effectively and accurately used. Data on past disasters and its critical analysis would help decision makers in formulating realistic and informed policy decisions and subsequent investments and implementations toward disaster prevention, mitigation, and preparedness. Capacity building should be encouraged at the local and regional levels for undertaking rapid-assessment surveys and investigations of the nature and extent of damage in postdisaster situations.

The use of information and communications technology (ICT) in disaster management in India is expected to reach $10 billion in 10 years. This fact was stated in a business conclave during the 58th International Astronautical Congress held in 2007. The global annual revenues of the ICT in the disaster management/geographic information system (GIS) market are expected to grow from an estimated $4 billion to $150 billion in the next decade (Detwiler 2016). With the increasing use of ICT (GIS) and high-resolution imagery services by government agencies, private companies, and individuals, the market is growing by leaps and bounds, and the advantages of the same should be appropriately utilized (Detwiler 2016).

References

Centre for Research on the Epidemiology of Disasters. 2017. *Emergency Disaster Database*. Brussels, Belgium: Centre for Research on the Epidemiology of Disasters.

Detwiler, J. 2016. *Geospatial Big Data Analytics*. University Park, PA: Penn State, College of Earth & Mineral Sciences.

Evans, J.R. 2016. *Business Analytics: Methods, Models and Decisions*. Upper Saddle River, NJ: Pearson, pp. 255–93.

Food and Agriculture Organization of the United Nations. 2015. *The Impact of Disasters on Agriculture and Food Security*. Rome, France: Food and Agriculture Organization of the United Nations, pp. 13–19.

United Nations. 2015. "Disaster Risk Reduction." Proceedings of Sendai-Japan Conference.

CHAPTER 3

Nuclear Disaster and Sustainability of Indian Agriculture

Rajesh Kumar

School of Social Sciences, Guru Nanak Dev University,
Amritsar, Punjab, India

Introduction

The Fukushima nuclear disaster, in 2011, destroyed a large number of farmhouses and fishing trawlers and also led to widespread radioactive contamination of soil, crops, and marine areas. It started fresh debates all over the world about the reliance of countries on nuclear power. The accident offered lessons to many countries, in general, and India, in particular. India is working on a plan to augment its existing nuclear power generation to 60,000 MWs by 2030 from a meager 3,500 MWs at present. It has 20 nuclear reactors that are functional, two that are nearing completion, and several new nuclear power plants that are at different stages of completion in its different states. While doing so, Indian policy makers need to bear in mind that despite technological advancements ensuring zero accidents at nuclear power plants, areas falling under mega nuclear power projects still remain prone to being struck by nuclear disasters. Any occurrence of a natural hazard-induced or man-made nuclear disaster in India will have serious ramifications for a large population that is dependent on agriculture. It is also likely to endanger food security for 75 percent of the country's rural population and 50 percent of the urban population (GOI-NFSA 2013). The pace at which new nuclear plants are being set up and becoming operational, the pros and cons of generating nuclear power, and the entire issue of linkages between development and environmental degradation because a nuclear disaster has a severe impact on agricultural and fishing communities residing in affected regions are being hotly debated. Serious concerns are being raised by policy makers all over the world. Several studies point out that operating a nuclear power reactor is never entirely free from risk and that mere assessments do not eliminate all risks, no matter how well the hazards have been assessed. The case of Fukushima 2011 is an eye-opener, confirming the premise that even advanced countries such as Japan could not prevent such disasters from occurring. Since Fukushima 2011, India too has begun witnessing long-standing protests at more than one of its nuclear power plants—Kudankulam, in the state of Tamil Nadu, and Jaitapur, in the state of Maharashtra. People in both states strongly fear the commissioning of new nuclear power plants as both states already have such plants that are functional.

In the era of global warming and climate change, the acceptability of nuclear power as a form of clean and green energy has increased. Thus, the dependence of countries, including India, on nuclear power has grown. India recently joined the United Nations Framework Convention on Climate Change (UNFCCC), concluded during the Paris Summit on October 2, 2016. For India, the decision to raise the content of nuclear power to overall electric power generation in the country is consistent with its international climate change obligations. Reports of International Panel on Climate Change (McCarthy and Canziani,-IPCC 2001)- point out that global warming and climate change have caused tsunamis and that Fukushima 2011 is an example of an earthquake-induced tsunami leading to nuclear disasters. In addition, any serious nuclear accident or exchange of nuclear warheads between countries during a war will raise the overall temperature of the atmosphere, thereby also contributing to global warming and climate change. It is because of the vicious nature of the relationship among different variables of nuclear disasters that the study on India's agricultural sustainability during nuclear disasters assumes significance.

As the Indian agricultural sector employs around 58 percent of the country's population, directly or indirectly, any natural hazard-induced nuclear disaster will have serious ramifications for the food security of a country with a population of 1.28 billion. Nuclear power generation and the heavy dependence of nations on it have always involved a number of risks pertaining to transportation of fissile material, reprocessing issues, safe storage, handling of nuclear waste, and other safety issues and threats posed to the local population. In the past few decades, the number of nuclear power plants has increased in India, and many more are being set up. In view of the recent natural disasters in the Indian states of Jammu and Kashmir and Uttarakhand, serious questions over the disaster handling capabilities and responsibilities of local state and federal governments were raised. They exposed many faults in their preparedness and largely proved that India still has a long way to go to match the state preparedness and disaster planning of Japan and other developed countries. Hence, the National Disaster Management Authority (NDMA) of India needs to bring its functioning more in tune with present realities, especially in dealing with nuclear disasters, which until now remains on paper only.

This chapter analyzes India's preparedness and capabilities of handling nuclear disasters and mitigating risks. The first section discusses reasons for India's increased dependence on nuclear energy, and the second section discusses reasons for likely nuclear disasters and handling capacities in postdisaster scenarios and their likely impact on agriculture and food security in the country. The last section discusses various shortcomings and future policy interventions. The methodology used is content analysis. A random sample survey, comprising a population of 350, was also conducted to test the general awareness among university students about nuclear disaster risks on a campus. The survey involved only 10 students from each of the 35 departments in a university. The chapter is based on the assumption that for a populated country like India, with limited exposure and a poor record of governments' handling of nonnuclear disasters in the past, managing the effects of nuclear disaster on agricultural production would be very difficult. The chapter's contribution to disaster management research is significant as it focuses on the role of education and dissemination of knowledge among the young people of India in building a culture of disaster-risk resilience.

Sources of Nuclear Disaster Risks in India

Climate Change Concerns and India's Nuclear Energy Program

India became a party to the Climate Change Agreement finalized during the Paris Summit on October 2, 2016. All countries, including India, are obliged to stop constructing new coal-fired power plants. As a result, India, in the last one and a half decades, has embraced nuclear energy for generating electricity. It is of the view that the cost of nuclear power can be reduced to that of coal-produced energy and that it will not affect climate change as it is considered clean and green energy.

India currently has seven nuclear power plants with 22 nuclear reactors (20 operational and two nearing completion), apart from research reactors at the Bhabha Atomic Research Centre (BARC), the Indira Gandhi Centre for Atomic Research (IGCAR), and other production-related establishments. They produce only around 4,700 MWe of electricity. Since the Indo-U.S. Nuclear Agreement of 2008, many new nuclear power plants have been coming up in different Indian states at places such as Jaitapur, in Maharashtra; Fatehabad, in Haryana; Haripur, in West Bengal; and in Andhra Pradesh, which is in line with the new energy policy of the Government of India (GOI) for generating approximately 60,000 MWe of electricity through the nuclear mode by 2032 (GOI-NPCIL 2014, p. 86). A report of the World Nuclear Association (WNA) says that India would be adding 20,000 MWe of nuclear capacity on line by 2020 and that it will reach 63,000 MWe by 2032. It will also raise the share of nuclear power in total power generation in the country to 25 percent by 2050(Schneider 2009). As discussed in the preceding section, India's international obligations of reducing its carbon emissions in order to prevent climate change, switching over to generation of electricity through the nuclear mode, is consistent with the signing of the UNFCC treaty and its recently announced policy under the Intentional Nationally Determined Contributions (INDC) at the Paris Summit on Climate Change in 2016.

Many scholars dispute that nuclear energy is a form of clean and green energy. The Report of Women in Europe for Common Future (WECF 2011), titled "Nuclear Power: The Critical Question," says that it is erroneous to consider nuclear energy a source of clean energy and has demanded a complete ban on the production of nuclear energy in Europe. This group even contradicts reports by the International Energy Agency (IEA) and the IPCC that global nuclear power generation would triple by 2050 and that it would save5 billion tons of carbon dioxide compared with a reduction of 25 to 40 billion tons by conventional methods by 2050. The WECF scholars and activists also have another fear: uranium, which is a limited resource, might be completely exhausted in the next 70 years (ibid.), and a switchover to thorium for fuel would result in dumping of a higher quantity of toxic nuclear waste on this planet as technology enables extraction of a larger quantity of plutonium using lesser plutonium as fuel inside fast breeder nuclear reactors (ibid.). The many complexities involved in nuclear power generation should urge a sense of prudence on the part of all countries, including India. It may be noted here that the debate about the pros and cons of nuclear energy acting as a source of clean and green energy is likely to dominate all future discourse in the coming decades.

Natural Hazards-Led Nuclear Disaster Threats at Nuclear Power Plants

A number of countries have experienced accidents at their nuclear sites because of natural hazards such as storms or tsunamis. The Fukushima 2011 nuclear disaster at the Daiichi plant occurred after it was hit by a tsunami. India too experienced an accident at the Kalpakkam nuclear plant in the aftermath of the 2004 tsunami. The ever-increasing concern with making India resilient to nuclear disasters from natural hazards and other types of disasters led to the setting up of an NDMA in India in 2005. The *National Disaster Management Guidelines: Management of Nuclear and Radiological Emergencies (NDMG-NRE)* of the GOI defines nuclear disaster as

> that dimension of emergency situation leading to mass casualties and destruction of large areas and property and the impact of a nuclear disaster that extends beyond the coping capability of local authorities demanding urgent handling at the national level including international assistance. (NDMG-NRE 2014, p. xxiv)

As discussed, experts continue to differ on issues of accepting nuclear power as a source of clean and carbon-free green energy. Nuclear scientists are of the view that 1 ton of uranium is sufficient to generate the same amount of electricity as 16,000 tons of coal burning and 80,000 barrels of oil (WECF 2011). It is a known fact that reprocessing of burnt fuel further yields uranium, plutonium, and nuclear waste. All nuclear power plants generate nuclear waste, and therefore the issue of safe handling and storage of nuclear toxic waste from nuclear power plants to disposal sites all over the world remains a challenging task for all countries, including India (Whittington and Laughten 2002, pp. 16535). Different countries have experienced recurring droughts, floods, storms, volcanoes, earthquakes, tsunamis, and landslides, also classified as natural hazards, that have been affecting their agricultural sector enormously. This kind of vulnerability remains very high in the world's second most populated country like India. Later sections of this chapter analyze the possibility of a nuclear disaster induced by a natural hazard like an earthquake-cum-tsunami in India, similar to what occurred in Fukushima, completely crippling agricultural crops because of radioactivity, thereby leading to a nuclear famine and causing millions of deaths.

Experts also remain divided on the possibility of disasters at nuclear power plants. While some believe such occurrences are impossible because of inbuilt foolproof safety systems that will ensure timely shutting down of the power plant others remain skeptical, seeing the main threat coming from nuclear power plants alone (Wilenius 1996). In the aftermath of the Fukushima nuclear disaster, countries and their experts concluded that Fukushima was the result of a natural hazard (earthquake-cum-tsunami) that completely destroyed three out of six of the Fukushima Daiichi nuclear power plants, leading to the toxic spread of radioactivity all over. According to the United Nations Scientific Committee on the Effects of Atomic Radiation Sixtieth session (May 2013) of UN General Assembly Report, "The Fukushima disaster led to a loss of 20,000 lives and destruction of unlimited property, infrastructure, and natural resources" (p. 7). Another report on the Fukushima nuclear disaster strongly emphasizes,

no country, developed or developing, is immune to such disasters. Advanced democracies are not necessarily more resistant or better prepared than developing countries to deal with such events. The Japanese experience thus offers many unique lessons for other democracies in terms of dealing with future disasters including India (Hasegawa 2013, pp. 22–35).

India's record in the handling of nuclear accidents so far has been fair. It was in 2004that the Madras nuclear power plant, at Kalpakkam, was struck by a tsunami, and a swift response ensured the successful stoppage of the nuclear reactor, averting a disaster (GOI-AERB 2005–2006, p. 58). However, the present era faces an increased threat of disaster in light of several new factors, discussed in the preceding and later sections. It is because of these factors that serious doubts have been cast on India's ability to handle a disaster on the scale of Fukushima.

Disaster Threats Caused by Accidental Nuclear War Risks and Nuclear Proliferation

Apart from threats to nuclear power plants arising from natural hazards, another possible factor is the outbreak of a nuclear war between countries. Such an outbreak within the Indian subcontinent can be sparked by, for instance, an accident, an error, or a malfunction or system failure. Even dissatisfied military generals could order a nuclear attack, or it could result from some miscalculations or from a country making use of the first strike policy against its enemy. Experts are of the view that threats regarding the use of such weapons by nonstate actors in the present era have increased considerably (Petras and Morley 1988). Going by the history of a strained relationship bedeviling two nuclear states (India and Pakistan) over the issue of Kashmir, the possibility of a nuclear war always remains.

An American think tank, Natural Resources Defense Council (NRDC), concluded:

a hypothetical nuclear exchange between India and Pakistan, in which each country targeted major cities through dozen, 25-kiloton warheads, 22.1 million people in India and Pakistan would be exposed to lethal radiation doses of 600 rem or more and 8 million people would receive a radiation dose of 100 to 600 rem, causing severe radiation sickness and potentially death, especially for the very young, old or infirm and as many as 30 million people would be threatened by the nuclear attack. NRDC estimated that 8.1 million people live within this radius of destruction. (NRDC 1998, pp. 497–510)

This threat persists even today with bigger manifestations of tension on the India–Pakistan border. The argument is strengthened by another report from the International Commission on Nuclear Non-Proliferation and Disarmament (ICNND) presented a decade ago before the United Nations, stating, "A nuclear war between India and Pakistan could cause severe 'climate cooling' and may have a devastating impact on agriculture worldwide." It added further,

the explosion of even a low-yield nuclear weapon in an urban or semi-urban area would cause massive loss of life, injury, sickness, and destruction due to the high population density and the concentration of high-value assets. They also represent an enormous and instantaneous loss of human and physical capital. (Evans and Kawaguchi, 2010)

All these reports sufficiently indicated the possibilities of large looming dangers of nuclear war in the Indian subcontinent, one of the most populous regions of the world.

According to a study by Toon et al. (2007) on fatalities of a possible nuclear war between India and Pakistan, "nuclear conflict would loft up to 6.6 Tg (6.6 tera grams or 6.6 million metric tons) of black carbon aerosol particles into the upper troposphere" (p. 1973). Another group of experts, Robock et al. (2007, p. 4), then calculated the effect that this injection of soot would have on the global climate if a war in South Asia were to occur in mid-May and confirmed "that a global average surface cooling of $-1.25°C$ persists for years." It found that even after a decade or so, the cooling was still $-0.50°C$. Further, the study found significant declines in global precipitation with marked decreases in rainfall in the most important temperate grain-growing regions of North America and Eurasia and a large reduction in the Asian summer monsoon (Robock et al. 2007, p. 4). Two additional studies, one by Stenke et al. (2013) and the other by Mills et al. (2013), also reached similar findings. According to these studies, both India and Pakistan remain vulnerable to the outbreak of a nuclear war between them, endangering the lives of several million people in the subcontinent.

The New Challenge of Terrorism

Post 9/11, the threat of a terrorist attack on nuclear power plants has increased considerably. To date, threats of terrorism have posed a serious challenge to security agencies that are commissioned to protect such installations and are meant to prevent such attacks from happening in any part of the world. These agencies always remain alert to attempted or planned attacks on nuclear power plants by nonstate actors who might try entering nuclear power plants or getting hold of nuclear material from them. Any security failure may enable terrorist organizations to succeed in exploding the nuclear reactors or in creating an unregulated nuclear chain reaction into the atmosphere, thus allowing radioactivity to spread all over. Another issue that merits attention here is the dilemma of nonstate actors who have the proper know-how for the making of nuclear devices after gaining access to fissile material, since nuclear devices cannot be made directly from uranium found in nature. Henceforth, terrorist organizations may try to get hold of an assembled nuclear device from a strategic storage point or may attempt to lift fissile material from a reprocessing plant's storage sites and may finally use a strategic material for a nuclear device. If this were ever to happen, the consequences would be unimaginable.

India, in recent years, has witnessed increased terrorist attacks on most secure places such as army camps/bases. Several such attacks in the state of Jammu and Kashmir have taken place in recent months, as late as in February 2018, when the Sunjuwaan army camp at Jammu was attacked by terrorists, leading to several causalities (*The Hindustan Times* 2018). In the light of increased attacks on army camps, the possibility of an attack on nuclear installations in India cannot be completely eliminated. Policy makers, as well as security agencies, ought to remain on high alert to forestall such attacks. Stronger measures therefore need to be taken and a road map prepared not only to reduce the threat of nuclear terrorism across the world but also to completely secure, augment, reduce, and, finally, dismantle nuclear devices and destroy strategic material from their stocks. Many countries, including India, have taken adequate steps to preempt such a threat (Nuclear Posture Review 2010).

According to the SIPRI 2017 report, "there are an estimated 4,150 nuclear weapons deployed throughout the world as on today, besides more than 10,785 nuclear weapons which are inactive, in reserve status, or awaiting demolition" (Kristensen 2017, p. 16). For the past several years, the international community have been expressing their concerns regarding the safety and security of nuclear weapons and materials in countries such as North Korea, Iran, Russia, Pakistan, and India. The role of the United Nations in expediting the process of concluding a nuclear weapons convention among member nations is to be greatly appreciated, in recognition of the fact that such dangers are escalating on a daily basis. The world, in recent years, has witnessed the dangers of nuclear war erupting between North Korea and the United States in late 2017 and early 2018. The international security scenario remains very grim because of the beginning of a new cold war era between the United States and Russia. The dependence of countries on nuclear weapons has increased considerably, confirming the results of studies carried out by various experts and nuclear disarmament activists (Kumar 2014, p. 151).

For the foregoing reasons, it is imperative that global public health policy makers remain committed to achieving the goals of nuclear disarmament at the earliest. Controlling the number of deaths in a heavily populated country such as India and saving billions of dollars' worth of property from damage through mishandling of a cask of spent fuel rods should always remain a priority for the GOI. Accordingly, the GOI has, in the last few years taken several measures such as raising more battalions of paramilitary forces, setting up of the National Investigation Agency (NIA), the National Intelligence Grid institutions; and also made the *Prevention of Unlawful Activities Act* more stringent after amendment. All such measures reflect the seriousness of the Indian federal government in dealing with terrorist threats. In times to come, countries will have to pool their energies in an effort to prevent nonstate actors from gaining control of nuclear assets of any country.

Impact of Nuclear Disaster on Agriculture

Scientists note that the entire area covering plants, land, rivers, seas, forests, or buildings in the vicinity of a nuclear plant would be contaminated the moment they came in contact with discharged/leaked radioactive material from a reactor. As a result, individuals, animals, and plants would be exposed to very severe radiation from these fissile materials (Winteringham 1989). Experts are firmly of the view that any excessive discharge of radioactive material into the environment would also contaminate food material such as fruits and vegetables (WHO-FAO 2011). Radionuclide elements may also be deposited on animal feed as deposits from the air, rain, or snow, thereby increasing the chances of radioactive contamination reaching up to an animal's intestines. All these effects would make it difficult for mankind to consume the milk given by these animals; even poultry products would be contaminated, rendering all such products purely unfit for consumption. The radioactivity in water resources too might reach the rivers and the sea, contaminating the flora and fauna therein. Radionuclide has a tendency to get easily deposited not only on flora and fauna but also on fish and seafood. Radionuclide material present in the atmosphere also has a tendency to enter into the food chain and, finally, get ingested by animals.

Scientists opine (WHO-FAO 2011) that in the aftermath of a nuclear accident, a variety of radionuclides would get released; some of them would be very short-lived, and some may not reach up to food. According to are port of the Food and Agriculture Organization (FAO), there are specific radioactive materials that impact negatively on the food chain. They include iodine (131I and 129I), cesium (134Cs and 137Cs), uranium (235U), plutonium (238Pu, 239Pu and 240Pu), cobalt (60Co), strontium (89Sr and 90Sr), radioactive hydrogen (3H), carbon (14C), technetium (99Tc), sulphur (35S), ruthenium (103Ru and 106Ru), cerium (103Ce), iridium (192Ir), and americium (241Am).

Not all radionuclides harm agriculture output. Iodine-131has a greater chance of entering into the food chain. Though experts say that iodine-131 has a short half-life and that it gets decomposed/decayed within a few weeks, it still manages to get quickly transferred from contaminated feed into milk, through which it enters the thyroid gland, damaging the tissues and causing cancer growth.

Some radioactive elements, such as cesium (Cs-134 and Cs-137), are very harmful to mankind as they do not decay quickly and have a half-life of two and thirty years, respectively. As a result, they remain present in the environment for a long time with a long-term impact on food material. Experts emphasize that strontium and plutonium, with a half-life of 29 and 24,100 years, respectively, are relatively immobile in the environment and are of local concern only, and may not cause a problem in international food trade. In the aftermath of Fukushima, it was noticed that with the passage of time, radioactivity could also build up within food and that radioactive particles reached crops or animals from soil or leached into rivers, lakes, and the sea, severely affecting fish and other seafood. Scientists (Johnson 2011) noticed that the coastal area of North Pacific Ocean too had traces of contamination.

Experts are of the view that the human body exposed to higher radiation remains prone to the development of cancer as these radioactive elements change the DNA structure within the body by harming the tissues. Any consumption of radioactive food material may lead to an increase in the health risks associated with radiation exposure. They also believe that contamination of crops, livestock, and agro-food products did take place because of a higher level of exposure at the Fukushima site. The FAO (2011) report on the impact of the Fukushima disaster on seafood safety highlights the massive contamination of the marine/coastal environment on account of the water used for cooling of the damaged reactors, which was highly contaminated after the leakage got mixed up with sea water. The highly contaminated radioactive water carrying contaminated soils was spread all over by rainwater runoffs. The report says that the radioactive material extended up to a distance of 10 km toward the Pacific from Fukushima (FAO 2011). In the Indian context, it is argued that nuclear plants in India are mostly located near coastal areas and that if a serious nuclear disaster breaks out, the possibility of the sea/marine environment getting contaminated remains very high.

Radioactive Elements Adjoining the Fukushima Marine Environment and Seafood

A study (Johnson 2011) carried out in the aftermath of the Fukushima disaster revealed many interesting facts for researchers and policy makers the world over. It found that cesium isotopes that have longer half-life covered longer distances by ocean currents and reached up to the Kuroshio current system. A lot of radioactive material got diluted in the abundant waters of the Pacific Ocean, reducing the danger considerably. The levels of Sr-90 and plutonium isotopes were very low as they are very heavy metals. The Japanese government, through its regulatory bodies, ensured that none of the marine contaminated products such as fish would be exported or allowed into local markets (Morino, Nishizawa, and Ohara 2011). Japanese fisheries agencies ensured that there were no health concerns pertaining to food sources by implementing stricter control measures for different radioactive elements in fish. The Japanese authorities constantly monitored the presence of I-131, Cs-134, and Cs-137 radioactive elements in food sources by picking up regular samples of seawater from 16 different sites (Fisheries Agency of Japan 2011). The alertness and commitment of Japanese officials in saving the lives of the multitudes of Japanese citizens have been exemplary (FAR Group 2011). Countries, including India, are following Japan's example by putting in place a similar kind of infrastructure for dealing with nuclear disasters.

Nuclear Disaster and Agricultural Sustainability in India

Issues and Challenges

The UN agencies regularly work for the dissemination of information among member countries aimed at turning their societies into one of disaster resilience. These agencies help member nations in exchanging a lot of information with each other and offer help to disaster-struck countries. The regular meeting of The United Nations Platform for Disaster Risk Reduction (UNPDRR) has been commendable. The UN's role has been instrumental in enabling the Indian government to take important strides toward the creation of a disaster-resilient society. According to the UN Report, more and more countries are affected by natural disasters such as floods threatening the livelihoods and food security of large populations. The FAO (2011) report cited in UNISDR (2015) stated that 815 million people globally are malnourished, nearly 14 percent of them in third world countries, and that 10.7 percent of the world's people suffer from chronic hunger (UNISDR 2015). Such reports draw our attention to the worldwide hunger problem because of an ever-increasing gap between the production of food grain and the number of starved, malnourished people in the world, especially in developing countries, including India.

As per the 2017 Global Hunger Index Report (Grebmer et al. 2017), approximately 300 million people in India go to bed without a second meal. A sizable rural population in India is dependent on agriculture, dairies, fisheries, forests, and livestock for their sustenance. India's record of handling flood disasters in recent years in states such as Bihar, Uttarakhand, Jammu and Kashmir, Assam, Maharashtra, or even Rajasthan has been far below international standards. Indian agriculture has been the worst affected sector from natural hazards and flood disasters, with a large portion of the population, comprising poor farmers and peasants or laborers, pushed further below the poverty line into deeper distress.

As mentioned, the FAO report 2014 highlighted that in the decade from 2003 to 2013, economic losses of an estimated $1.5 trillion have taken place because of natural disasters the world over. The losses to developing countries, with an estimated 2 billion victims, totaled $550 billion (FAO 2014). The Human Cost of Weather-Related Disasters 1995–2015 reported 6,457 weather-related disasters in the decade from 1995 to 2015, which killed approximately 600,000 people (UNISDR 2015).

For India, with a population of 1.28 billion, one of the main objectives of food management has been to maintain adequate reserves for food security and avoid any price instability in the country. It is because of the grim food availability scenario that India's *National Food Security Act 2013*, under the Targeted Public Distribution System, aims to cover almost 50 percent of urban and 75 percent of rural populations needing subsidized food grains (Government of India 2013).The gravity of the hunger problem in India can be gauged from several facts and figures provided by different national and international agencies through their reports on a regular basis. For these reasons, a serious debate on India's increased dependence on nuclear power, which remains prone to the occurrence of nuclear disasters, is of relevance to food security in the contemporary era.

All past and present governments in India have remained sensitive to the need to address the hunger problem of the country. In tune with the objective of achieving sustainability in the agricultural sector, the GOI has been continuing programs such as *National Food Security Mission* since 2007 and *National Mission for Sustainable Agriculture and National Horticulture Mission*. With a view to ushering in the second green revolution in the country, the GOI has also been implementing *Rashtriya Krishi Vikas Yojna* since 2007, with a commitment to double the income of farmers by 2022 to provide a big economic boost to make farming more viable. Under the 11th Five Year Plan (2007–2012) and the 12th Five Year Plan (2012–2017), the GOI continually emphasizes a 4 percent growth rate per annum in the gross domestic report (GDP) from farming and miscellaneous sectors. However, growth has remained close to only 3.6 percent. For the past one and a half decades, India has been facing a serious agrarian crisis because of the deaths, in different parts of the country, of around half a million farmers burdened by financial debts. For a large section of farmers, cultivation has degenerated into a highly nonprofitable venture.

As discussed, the contribution of agriculture and allied sectors in the country's gross domestic product was around 14 percent, whereas the share of agriculture in providing employment, according to the 2011 Census, has been 58 percent (GOI-Year Book 2017). The Indian states of Punjab and Haryana are always exposed to the threat of a nuclear disaster because of the strained India–Pakistan relationship, and, in view of their proximity to Pakistan, are expected to bear the brunt of any war that erupts between the two countries. Any outbreak of war with Pakistan will have a severe bearing on the country's agricultural production as Punjab and Haryana are a major source of the entire country's food supply. These two neighboring states play a crucial role in achieving India's national food security goals.

As discussed in the preceding sections, Indian agriculture has been a victim of natural hazards such as droughts, storms, floods, and landslides, which have taken a heavy toll on a recurring basis, thereby turning agriculture into one of India's most vulnerable sectors. Every year, the monsoon brings floods to north and central India, and states such as Bihar, Assam, Bengal, Gujarat, and Andhra Pradesh are known to be hugely affected. The year 2017 was a particularly bad year for Bihar, Assam, and Rajasthan, which experienced the worst floods in the country (GOI-NDMA 2017). On the whole, Indian agriculture has been impacted by a number of natural calamities all over the country, registering colossal losses. Food prices have been rising globally in the 21st century, thwarting India's achievement of its food security goals. The price rises have been as high as 40 percent since mid-2007, and the prices of staple food grains have increased by 80 percent. This distressing global trend has put the agricultural sector under pressure to transform itself so as to overcome the food shortage and, ultimately, guarantee food security worldwide. In response to the food security threat, the incumbent Indian government, led by Prime Minister Narendra Modi, increased the minimum support prices of monsoon crops by one and a half times in June 2018 so as to increase the farmers' annual total income and arrest the trend of their suicidal deaths. The GOI is committed to doubling the annual income of farmers by 2022 (GOI-BUDGET 2018–19).

Thus, it is clear that Indian agriculture, which is already grievously affected by the foregoing factors, cannot withstand any further disaster-like scenarios.

FAO's Concerns about World Food Security

The goal of zero hunger and world food security is also important from the point of view of SDGs (20152030). The UN Food and Agriculture Organization June 2013 Report has raised concern about the inadequate availability of food grain throughout the world in the coming years, estimating the world grain stocks at 509 million metric tons (FAO 2013), or close to only 1/5 of the total annual consumption of 2,339 million metric tons. The report said that at the current level, food grain stock may last only 77 days in case of emergencies (FAO 2013). Third-world countries, including India, are likely to be more affected on this account. According to another report of the US Department of Agriculture, "there are 432 million metric tons of grain stocks, which is about 19% of total annual consumption of 2,289 million metric tons sufficient to last for 68 days only" (USDA Census of Agriculture, 2012). The same report also estimated that around 870 million people are suffering from malnutrition (ibid.). On the basis of facts and figures furnished by various other reports, it may be observed that any further drop in food production because of climate change and natural disasters would have disastrous consequences for the world, in general, and India in particular.

Experts' studies on the effects of a tactical nuclear war on agricultural production and food prices reveal that with the rise in food prices, there would be an annual decline in food production, which would force 40 million people to remain malnourished. One study estimated that in the next 10years around 215 million people would suffer malnourishment. It added that a 20 percent annual decline in crop yield would increase crop prices by 19.7 percent. Finally, it forecast that a nonuniform price rise would be witnessed globally. For example, prices in South Asia were to rise by 31.6 percent as against21.4 percent in East Asia (Helfand 2013). All such findings raise serious questions over the issue of agricultural sustainability in India and point to grave food security issues in the event of a nuclear war in South Asia.

Another study on the impact of a nuclear disaster on agriculture, by the Radiological Protection Institute of Ireland (RPII), noted that "there are currently over 400 nuclear power plants in operation across the world, of which 185 are in Europe" (RPII—McMahon 2014, p.1). A severe accident at any one of these plants could lead to radioactive contamination reaching Ireland, the amount depending on the severity of the accident and prevailing weather conditions (ibid.). It noted further that in the event of a nuclear accident, there is a larger risk of radiation, as much as 90 percent, from the consumption of contaminated food alone. The RPII report categorically asserts that risks of radiation doses can be reduced if the right kinds of agricultural management techniques and food control methods are adopted. The effects of postaccident/disaster radiation may last for several months or years depending on its severity. News of fresh cases of contamination related to the Fukushima disaster keeps surfacing even in 2018 (Farrell 2018). The best practices mentioned in the RPII study are also relevant to India and are discussed in a later section.

Although India does have an elaborate plan, as mentioned in the NDMG-NRE document, for the handling of nuclear disasters in the country (Government of India NDMG-NRE 2009), it needs to work seriously on many areas and adopt new measures for mitigating such disaster risks and achieving a more disaster risk-resilient society. The risk remains very high in the South Asian subcontinent, where three nuclear weapon states, namely, India, Pakistan, and China, share common land boundaries with each other. India and China have, in recent years, emerged as bigger nuclear players by laying greater emphasis on the use of nuclear energy. Both India and Pakistan are trying their best to acquire membership in the Nuclear Suppliers Group (NSG) so that their participation in nuclear commerce may increase at the international level. The consequences of an India–Pakistan nuclear war are briefly discussed in earlier sections. The consequences of an India–China nuclear war are beyond the purview of this chapter.

Fukushima Nuclear Disaster, EU Strategies, and Lessons for Indian Agriculture

Food self-sufficiency has always remained a priority for India, an agrarian country, where approximately 58 percent of the population is dependent on agriculture for direct or indirect employment. However, the contribution of agriculture and allied sectors in the country's GDP remains close to only 14 percent. Like Japan, India gives food security policy high priority in its governance. India's dependence on food security is much higher than Japan's as India is the second most populated country in the world. The FAO (2013) report, discussed in the preceding section, highlighted concerns about the precarious food security conditions in South Asia. As discussed earlier, Japan witnessed massive devastation of mainly agricultural and fishery areas after the Fukushima earthquake and tsunami in 2011. The Congressional Research Service (CRS) report of May 2011 estimated a total loss of $21.5 billion in damages to Japan's agriculture, fisheries, and forestry after it was hit by those disasters (Johnson 2011). Japan and India share several topographical similarities as both countries have vast coastal areas. In the event of a nuclear disaster, India's fisheries, agriculture, and forestry sectors would suffer colossal losses as its coastline extends up to 7,500 km (GOI 2017, p. 371). Most of the Indian nuclear power plants are in the coastal states of Maharashtra, Karnataka, Tamil Nadu, Gujarat, and Andhra Pradesh, which have significant fishery areas.

Following the pattern of EU countries, India needs to train its population on the contents of the RPII and the Ireland Government's handbook (RPII 2010), which outlines actions that will reduce or eliminate the transfer of radioactive fallout to the food chain following a nuclear emergency and ensure that all food on sale is safe to eat. However, as noted in the NDMG-NRE Guidelines, to deal with nuclear and radio-logical disasters, there are important instructions for the people and all other stakeholders. Following the pattern of the RPII, India also needs to develop strategies, guidance, and tools for the management of contam-inated goods, including food and animal feed. The RPIIEU project lays particular emphasis on inclusion of the views of producers, processors, re-tailers, and consumers in the process, and this is of considerable relevance to India too. As in Ireland, all Indian state governments have a statutory obligation to establish a State Disaster Management Authority (SDMA) as well as a District Disaster Management Authority (DDMA). These bodies are designed to mitigate disaster risks and move in the direction of being a disaster-resilient society. India needs to continue to emulate the EU practices of involving all national stakeholder panels. Panels have been established in India after the pattern of those in European countries. These panels include a wide range of stakeholders who are supposed to meet several times to share their experiences of dealing with real and per-ceived contaminated products, impacts on trade, and the implementation of control measures.

Respondents' Perceptions of Disaster Management

A random sample survey was conducted to test the general awareness among university students of nuclear disaster risks in Amritsar district of Indian Punjab, involving a population of 350. The random sample survey involved only ten students from each of the 35 departments in the university. Students were supplied with a printed questionnaire and were chosen by the authors visiting different departments on different occa-sions without segregating male and female students.

The following questions were asked:

Q.1. Name the body responsible for disaster management in India.
Q.2. Who holds the disaster management responsibility at the state/district level in India?
Q.3. Do you know about the latest disaster management act in India?
Q.4. Are you aware of the hazards your district is prone to?
Q.5. Do you know how many nuclear reactors India possesses?

Q.6. Are you aware of the harmful effects of radiation from a nuclear disaster and what it actually does to our bodies and the environment?

Q.7. Do you feel that nuclear power generation poses more risk than benefit to society?

Q.8. Do you know about the Chernobyl nuclear disaster?

Q.9. Do you know about the Three Mile Island nuclear accident?

Q.10. Are you aware of the Fukushima Daiichi nuclear disaster and its impact on agriculture?

Findings of a Survey Conducted on Respondents by the Author

The valid responses of students are summarized in Table 3.1. This survey did not make use of any statistical tools as the study was merely of a preliminary nature (a pilot test).

Table 3.1 Nuclear disaster management awareness among respondents

Question	Unsure	Fully aware	Who said YES	Partially aware	No awareness at all	Did not give any response	Total respondents who answered questions serially
Q.1	58	52	46	18	24	114	312
Q.2	74	36	38	04	24	134	310
Q.3	32	—	54	04	122	82	294
Q.4	16	—	170	20	46	42	294
Q.5	98	10	48	—	76	50	282
Q.6	—	10	226	34	20	24	314
Q.7	16	—	204	—	58	32	310
Q.8	—	—	102	—	168	40	310
Q.9	—	—	70	—	196	48	314
Q.10	—	04	130	—	124	42	300

Source: Author conducted a survey of 350 university students in summer 2017.

It can be inferred from the responses to Questions 1 to 3 in Table 3.1 that only 52 out of 350 university students were fully aware of the existence of disaster mechanisms such as NDMA, SDMA, and DDMA in the country. It was shocking to discover that not a single student knew about the existence of the DDMA in Amritsar district of Punjab, where the university is located. It clearly showed that the educated youth of Amritsar city were least concerned about the chances of a nuclear conflict leading to a nuclear disaster. They thought it would never occur on the India–Pakistan border, especially in the Amritsar district of Punjab situated just 20 miles away from the Pakistani border. Despite the inclusion of disaster-related topics in the curriculum of the Environment course (a compulsory paper for undergraduates across disciplines), the majority of the students did not know about nuclear disasters clearly demonstrating their apathy toward serious social issues.

In regard to Question 4, more than 50 percent (170 out of 294) of the students were aware of nuclear hazards but not the mechanisms available for disaster handling that were in place in their towns. This meant that only half of the students knew that India and Pakistan are nuclear powers and that if a war broke out between them, these nuclear weapons can cause havoc to cities such as Amritsar.

On Question 5, regarding the total number of reactors set up in different parts of the country, only 10 out of 282 students (less than 0.5 percent) were fully aware of the 20 nuclear reactors that are functional in India.

About 226 out of 314 (72 percent) students said that they had heard about the harmful impact of nuclear radiation, referred to in Question 6. This meant that the majority of students understood the consequences of radioactivity.

Around two-thirds (204 out of 310) of the respondents agreed that nuclear power generation poses more risks than benefits to society (Question 7). This showed that the Fukushima disaster may have been a factor that instilled fear within the minds of some of the youth about the dangers of increased dependence on nuclear power. Further research would be needed to uncover all the factors that led to that result.

Responding to Question 8, close to 200 out of 310 respondents did not know about the Chernobyl nuclear disaster at all. Around 250 out of 314 respondents knew nothing about the Three Mile Island nuclear accident in the United States the subject of Question 9.

Lastly, only one-third of the respondents (130 out of 300) knew about the Fukushima Daiichi nuclear disaster of 2011, which figured in Question 10. Taken together, these three questions showed that the youth on campus lacked awareness of the history of nuclear accidents anywhere in the world. They lacked interest in historical facts, although pertaining to the 1970s, and as many as two-thirds of the students did not know about the Fukushima disaster of 2011. This showed that the majority of the students were less concerned about societal and environmental issues and that they believed more in present rather than future threats to societies.

On the whole, policy makers ought to bear in mind that no disaster risk-resilient society can be built without community participation and without the involvement of youth. This survey is an eye-opener to the fact that urgent measures need to be taken to involve Indian youth on a much larger scale and that their symbolic involvement in NCC (National Cadet Corps), NSS (National Service Scheme), and similar other activities may not avail in the event of nuclear emergencies. As long as it happens and unless more effective steps are taken, preparedness for mitigating nuclear disaster risks in India will remain incomplete, validating the author's fear, expressed at the outset, that most of the nuclear disaster handling preparedness exists on paper only.

Conclusion

To conclude, India needs to tread carefully in implementing its ambitious nuclear power program, in the light of its needs and realistic capabilities in managing nuclear disasters. The Indian federal government must fine-tune its energy policy in light of the post-Fukushima disaster and prioritize the tapping of the vast potential of solar and wind energy on a much larger scale. The idea of reducing its dependence on nuclear energy must be ingrained in all of its future energy policy making. Though considerable euphoria was generated in India over the signing of the US–India Nuclear Agreement of 2008, it stands empty a decade later in 2018. Hardly any new reactors have been fully established anywhere in the country 0years after the agreement. India's *Nuclear Liability Act 2010*, just before the Fukushima disaster, has discouraged the supply of nuclear reactors from many foreign sources to India. Meantime, India is today faced with more resistance from the people, making it very difficult for federal and state governments to acquire land from farmers for mega national projects, including construction of new nuclear power plants in India. Thus, the realization of the goal of generating 60,000MWs of electricity through the nuclear mode by 2030 seems to be elusive, if not impossible. The need of the hour is to take adequate steps to make agriculture more sustainable in India. At the end of the second decade of the 21st century, the agricultural sector is passing through one of the worst stages in the history of independent India. Any harm to Indian agriculture on account of natural hazard-led nuclear disasters will precipitate a hunger crisis beyond one's imagination.

India needs to ensure that after a nuclear emergency all food on sale would be safe to eat. To do this, India must, after the manner of the EU countries, train its population to follow the NDMG-NRE Guidelines, which outline actions that will reduce or eliminate the transfer of radioactive fallout along the food chain. The NDMA Guidelines deal with nuclear and radiological disasters and carry important instructions for the people and all other stakeholders. These guidelines need to be communicated to the people on a regular basis by conducting periodic drills in preparation for such disasters. A joint training exercise with the help of National Disaster Response Force (NDRF) specialists for the citizens of Amritsar, Punjab, and other border towns of the country should be conducted regularly to create a large pool of trained personnel to undertake disaster relief work anywhere in the country. The supply of medicines to be administered in the aftermath of a nuclear disaster should be augmented in all government-run hospitals. Other necessary equipment and special protective gear should be procured and kept ready by the government and district agencies at all times. India also needs to develop strategies, guidance, and tools for the management of contaminated goods, including food and animal feed, by involving all stakeholders on a regular basis. Introducing courses on disaster management in universities/colleges is a must. The involvement of youth in disaster-related tasks should be undertaken on a very large scale, in line with the survey findings cited earlier. There is an urgent need for developing a new culture of resilience toward such disasters among the common citizens/farmers/laborers. The federal GOI needs to encourage the state governments to prepare themselves in light of the current realities. The youth of the country need to be motivated toward creating an exclusive corps of volunteers who would remain ever ready to offer their services at critical times following the pattern of the NCC and the NSS. The private sector will also need to assume a major responsibility for such causes. A special disaster tax on patterns of education or a tax on petrol can be imposed with a view to creating a fund to support education and training of youth and human resources exclusively for disaster-related needs.

References

Evans, G., and Y. Kawaguchi. 2010. "Report of the International Commission on Nuclear Non-Proliferation and Disarmament." *Eliminating Nuclear Threats: A Practical Agenda for Global Policy Makers.* Canberra, Australia. http://www.icnnd.org/reference/reports/ent/index.html

Farrell, J. 2018. "Fukushima Nuclear Disaster: Lethal Levels of Radiation Detected in Leak Seven Years after Plant Meltdown in Japan." *The Independent.* https://www.independent.co.uk/news/world/asia/fukushima-nuclear-disaster-radiation-lethal-leak-japan-tsunami-tokyo-electric-power-company-a8190981.html

Food and Agriculture Organization. 2011. *FAO Annual Report 2011.* http://www.fao.org/docrep/014/am719e/am719e00.pdf

Food and Agriculture Organization. 2013. *FAO Annual Report 2013.* http://www.fao.org/3/a-i3887e.pdf

Food and Agriculture Organization. 2014. *FAO Annual Report 2014.* http:/www.fao.org/publications/sofa/2014/en.pdf Government of India. 2005–2006. *Atomic Energy Regulatory Board Annual Report.* Bombay: AERB.

Government of India. 2015. *NPCIL Annual Report. 2014-15.* http:www.npcil.nic.in/content/514_1_AnnualReports.aspx Government of India. 2017. *Year Book.* New Delhi: Government of India.

Government of India. 2018. *Annual Budget 2018-19.* https://www.indiabudget.gov.in/ub2018-19/bs/bs.pdf

Government of India, Ministry of Law and Justice. 2013. *National Food Security Act.* https://www.egazette.nic.in/WriteReadData/2013/E_29_2013_429.pdf

Government of India. NDMA. 2009. *National Disaster Management Guidelines-Nuclear and Radiological Emergencies (NDMG-NRE)*, February 2014, p. xxiv. https://ndma.gov.in/en/ndma-guidelines.html

Grebmer, K.V., J. Bernstein, T. Bron, N. Prasai, & Y. Yohannes. 2017. *Global Hunger Index: The Inequalities of Hunger.* www.globalhunger-index.org

Hasegawa, R. 2013. *Disaster Evacuation from Japan's 2011 Tsunami Disaster and the Fukushima Nuclear Accident.* IDDRI, Tokyo, Japan. https://www.iddri.org/sites/default/files/import/publications/study/0513_rh_devast-report.pdf

Helfand, I. 2013. *Nuclear Famine: Two Billion People at Risk?* https:www.psr.org/wp-content/uploads/2018/04/two-billion-at-risk.pdf

Johnson, R. 2011. *Japan's 2011 Earthquake and Tsunami: Food and Agriculture Implications.* Washington, DC: CRS. https://fas.org/sgp/crs/row/R41766.pdf

Kennedy, E. 2010. *Ireland Government's Handbook 2010.* Radiological Protection Institute of Ireland (RPII). https://www.epa.ie/pubs/reports/other/corporate/rpII/ar2009/AR_23_166AnnualReport09EN.pdf

Kristensen, H.M. 2017. "Status of World Nuclear Forces 2017." In *SIPRI Year Book 2017.* Stockholm, Sweden: Oxford University Press. https://www.sipri.org/yearbook/2017/11

Kumar, R. 2014. "Emerging Threats of Nuclear Terrorism: Issues and Challenges." In *Threats to India's Internal Security*, eds. R. Prasad and S.C. Pandey. New Delhi: Mohit Publications.

McCarthy, J.J., and O.F. Canziani, eds. 2001. *IPCC Report 2001: Climate Change 2001: Impacts, Adaptation and Vulnerability, Contribution of Working Group II to the Third Assessment Report of IPCC.* https://www.preventionweb.net/files/8387_wg2TARfrontmatter1.pdf

McMahon, C. 2014. *Radiological Protection Institute of Ireland (RPII) News Brief.* https://www.epa.ie/pubs/reports/radiation/RPII_Radiation_Doses_Irish_Population_2014.pdf

Mills, M., O.B. Toon, J. Taylor, and A. Robock. 2013. "Multi-Decadal Global Cooling and Unprecedented Ozone Loss Following a Regional Nuclear Conflict." In *Nuclear Famine: Two Billion People At Risk?*, eds. I. Helfand. International Physicians for the Prevention of

Nuclear War, Physicians for Social Responsibility. http://www.atmos-chem-phys-discuss.net/13/12089/2013/acpd-13-12089-2013.html

Ministry of Agriculture, Forestry and Fisheries. 2011. "The Damages caused by the Great East Japan Earthquake and Actions taken by Ministry of Agriculture, Forestry and Fisheries." In *Japan's 2011 Earthquake and Tsunami: Food and Agriculture Implications,* eds. R. Johnson. Reported at 1,752.2 billion yen, *Congressional Research Service,* 7-5700. http://www.maff.go.jp/e/quake/press_110511-1.html (accessed May 18, 2011).

Morino, Y., M. Nishizawa, and T. Ohara. 2011. "Atmospheric Behavior Deposition, and Budget of Radioactive Materials from the Fukushima Daiichi Nuclear Power Plant in March 2011." *Geophysical Research Letters 38,* L00GII. doi:10.1029/2011GL048689.

NRDC Report and Louis Ren Beres. 1998. "In a Dark Time: The Expected Consequences of an India-Pakistan Nuclear War." *American University of International Review* 14, no. 1, pp. 497–510.

Petras, J., and M. Morley. 1988. "Nuclear War and US-Third World Relations: The Neglected Dimension." *Economic and Political Weekly* 23, no. 4, pp. 151–8. http://www.jstor.org/stable/4378015 (accessed March 8, 2011).

Rabobank Food and Agribusiness Research and Advisory (FAR) Group. March, 2011. "Japan Earthquake: Magnitude of Impact on Food and Agriculture." *Kiplinger Agriculture Letter.*

Robock, A., L. Oman, G.L. Stenchikov, B. Owen, C. Toon, C. Bardeen, and P.T. Richard. 2007. "Climatic consequences of regional nuclear conflicts." *Atmospheric Chemistry and Physics* 7, pp. 2003–2012.

Schneider, M. 2009. *World Nuclear Industry Status Report (WNISR).* www.world-nuclear.org/info/inf53.html

Stenke, A. 2013. "Climatic consequences of regional nuclear conflicts." *Atmospheric Chemistry and Physics* 7, pp. 9713-9714. https://www.atmos-chem-phys.net/13/9713/2013/acp-13-9713.2013.pdf

The Hindustan Times, Jalandhar: 13 February 2018. https://m.hindustantimes.com/punjab/jalandhar

The Times of India, Chandigarh: 26 January 2010. https://timesofindia.indiatimes.com/archive/year-2010, month-1.cms

Toon, O.B., B.R. Owen, W.A. Robock, R.P. Turco, C. Bardeen, L. Oman, G.L. Stenchikov, 2007. "Nuclear War- consequences of regional scale nuclear conflicts." *Science* 315, no. 5816, pp. 1224–25. http://climate.envsci.rutgers.edu/pdf/SciencePolicyForumNW.pdf

U.S. Department of Defense. April, 2010. *Nuclear Posture Review Report.* https://dod.defense.gov/Portals/1/features/defenseReviews/NPR/2010_Nuclear_Posture_Review_Report.pdf

UN Report on Agriculture and Disaster Risk. 2011. "A Contribution by the United Nations to the Consultation Leading to the Impact on Seafood Safety of the Nuclear Accident in JAPAN—9 May 2011." WHO, FAO. http://www.jfa.maff.go.jp/e/inspection/index.html

UNGA. 2013. "Report of the United Nations Scientific Committee on the Effects of Atomic Radiation Sixtieth Session (27–31 May 2013)." General Assembly Official Records Sixty-eighth Session, Supplement No. 46, pp. 9–10. https://research.un.org/en/docs/ga/quick/regular/68

United Nations Office for Disaster Risk Reduction (UNISDR). 2015. *Proceedings: Third UN World Conference on Disaster Risk Reduction.* 14–18 March 2015. https://www.wcdrr.org/preparatory

United States Department of Agriculture, 2012. *2012 Census of Agriculture.* https://www.nass.usda.gov/Publications/AgCensus/2012/highlights

WECF Report. 2011. *Nuclear Power: The Critical Question.* http://www.wecf.eu/english/publications/2011/critical-questionsnuclear.php

Whittington, B., and M. Laughten, eds. 2002. "Our Energy Future? A Commentary on The PIU'S Energy Review." *Energy and Environment* 13, no. 1. pp. 1653–68.

WHO-FAO. March, 2011. "Nuclear accidents and radioactive contamination of foods." *News Brief.* https://www.who.int/foodsafety/fs_management/radionuclides_and_food_300311.pdf

Wilenius, M. 1996. "From Science to Politics: The Menace of Global Environmental Change." *Acta Sociologica* 39, no.1, pp. 5–30. http://www.jstor.org/stable/4194803 (accessed March 8, 2011).

Winteringham, F.P.W. 1989. *Radioactive Fallout in Food and Agriculture.* IAEA-TECDOC-494. Vienna, Austria: IAEA.

Wright, T. 2010. *Towards Nuclear Abolition: NPT Review Conference 2010.* Article 36 is part of the International Steering Group of the International Campaign to Abolish Nuclear Weapons (ICAN). http://www.icanw.org/wp-content/uploads/2012/08/nptrevcon2010.pdf

CHAPTER 4

Building Resilience to Natural Disasters: Toward Sustainable Agricultural Practices in Sri Lanka

R. Lalitha S. Fernando
M.S. Dimuthu Kumari
W.M.D.M. Dissanayaka

Department of Public Administration, University of Sri Jayewardenepura, Nugegoda, Sri Lanka

Background of the Study and Problem Identification

The agriculture sector remains the backbone of many rural economies. (According to the World Bank (2017a), the agricultural sector contributes 4 percent to global gross domestic product (GDP) and around 26 percent to the GDP of many least developed countries. Also, the population directly involved in agriculture is significant. By 2017, the figure is about 26.81 percent at the global level and 60 percent from least developed countries (World Bank 2017b). Normally, the agricultural sector is badly affected by natural disasters, particularly from floods and drought.

According to the United Nations International Strategy for Disaster Reduction (2013), during the period 1980 to 2011, 3,455 flood situations, 2,689 storms, 470 droughts, and 395 extreme temperature situations were recorded worldwide. According to the International Federation of Red Cross and Red Crescent societies (2016), the total number of natural disasters reported during the period 2005 to 2015 worldwide is as follows: 2,556-Asia; 1,522-Africa; 1,242-America; 846-Europe; and 147-Oceanian continent.

The Food and Agriculture Organization (FAO) of the United Nations has noted that Asia is the most affected region, its estimated losses to the agricultural sector totaling $28 billion. A generic trend is that damage and losses from mega disasters in agriculture are higher in countries where the contribution of agriculture to GDP is still high and where agriculture provides a main source of employment. Both characteristics feature high in LDCs (UN World Conference on Disaster Risk Reduction, 2015).

The agricultural sector in Sri Lanka is considered a major economic force in the country, contributing significantly to the national economy, food security, and employment. More than 70 percent of the population lives in rural areas, engaging in agriculture for their livelihoods (Department of Agriculture 2016). Currently, the agricultural sector accounts for about 7.1 percent of the GDP and 27.1 percent of employment (CBSL 2016). Rice is the staple food of the inhabitants of Sri Lanka, and paddy is cultivated as a wetland crop in all the districts. According to the Sri Lanka paddy statistics (2016), the total amount of land devoted to paddy is estimated to be 708,000 hectares at present. There are two cultivation seasons, based on two monsoons (Yala and Maha), which bring rain for cultivation. The Maha season falls during the northeast monsoon, from September to March. The Yala season extends from May to the end of August.

Floods, drought, landslides, and lightning are frequent disasters in Sri Lanka.

By April 2014, the Department of Agriculture reported that lack of rain has damaged 83,746 hectares of paddy planted area resulting in an estimated production loss of 280,000 MT of rice (15 per cent of forecasted production) (United Nations Office for the Coordination of Humanitarian Affairs 2014).

During the past 10 years, Sri Lanka has faced 23 occurrences of flooding, in which over 500 lives were lost and 9 million people affected, according to the International Water Management Institute (2014).

These floods caused an economic loss of $41 billion (United Nations Office for the Coordination of Humanitarian Affairs 2014). The Department of Agriculture reported that lack of rain damaged 83,746 hectares of paddy-planted areas, resulting in an estimated production loss of 280,000 metric tons (MT) of rice (United Nations Office for the Coordination of Humanitarian Affairs 2014). Many households in the disaster-affected areas engage in small-scale farming activities. The damages are also reported in the livestock sector. According to the Statistics of the Department of Animal Production and Health (2014), over 19,900 cases of foot-and-mouth disease among the livestock were reported from 18 districts (United Nations Office for the Coordination of Humanitarian Affairs 2014) after flooding. Around 75,000 families have been affected by a flood that occurred in Sri Lanka in May 2016 (Disaster Management Information System in Sri Lanka 2016).

When natural disasters occur, the poor are the most vulnerable segment of society. According to the World Bank (2016), 78 percent of the world's poor live in rural areas and depend largely on farming for their survival. The United Nations Food and Agricultural Organization (2015) also noted that disasters have a direct impact on the livelihoods and food security of millions of small farmers, pastoralists, fisheries, and forest-dependent communities in developing countries. The poor in the rural sector engaged in agriculture are, unsurprisingly, helpless in the face of disasters, and is imperative to ensure their survival and improve their living conditions through sustainable agricultural practices.

The impact of disasters could be seen as various forms such as loss of harvest and livestock, irrigation systems and other agricultural infrastructure, contamination of water bodies and also spreading various diseases.

According to the FAO (2015), the agricultural sector accounts for about 22 percent of the total damage caused by natural disasters, particularly in developing countries. Further, disasters transform the agricultural trade flows and also the agriculture-based manufacturing subsectors because of the frequent fluctuations in the supply side of agricultural products. Most significantly, natural hazards weaken economic growth in many developing countries. However, the FAO (2015) commented that mainstreaming disaster risk reduction into the agricultural sector is inadequate. Despite their national platforms, policies, and legislation, only a few countries address agriculture-related issues in disaster situations. Therefore, it is time to rethink existing agricultural policies, particularly in developing countries and analyze them to identify policy gaps.

It has been observed that the existing agricultural policy in Sri Lanka has been, to some extent, enriched with several components but that these have not been adequately considered during implementation. This chapter thus aims to identify issues of policy implementation. The main objectives of this study are to identify the strengths and weaknesses of existing agricultural policy in Sri Lanka and to propose the best strategies to cope with disasters by examining good practices in other countries. Agricultural policies should be sustainable even during disasters. This study assumes significance in that its recommendations would be useful in designing and maintaining a sustainable agriculture policy for Sri Lanka.

Methodology

A qualitative approach based on secondary data was employed. Best practices of sustainable agricultural policies of select countries were reviewed. Government circulars, newspaper and journal articles, and e-sources were used as secondary data. Thematic analysis with substantial description was used to analyze the data. A method of policy analysis proposed by Dunn (2016) and an approach proposed by Hoogwood and Gunn (1984) were used mainly to analyze agricultural policy in Sri Lanka. This study selected the retrospective strategy suggested by Dunn (2016). This strategy consists of three aspects—a discipline-oriented approach, a problem-oriented approach, and an application-oriented approach. The problem-oriented approach was the main focus of the study, identifying issues in the implementation of the policy. Content analysis and process analysis, proposed by Hoogwood and Gunn (1984), were used to analyze Sri Lankan agricultural policy.

Literature Review on Agriculture and Disasters

This section discusses related concepts of disasters and agriculture and also relevant literature on policy analysis. Selected best policies and practices related to sustainable agricultural policies and related empirical research are also presented.

Disaster Resilience

According to the United Nations Office for Disaster Risk Reduction (UNISDR 2005), the term disaster resilience is used to describe the capacity of any individual, organization, or country that can make the required adjustments and progress despite the damages and shocks of disasters, without sacrificing its future development aspirations. Also, Hyogo Framework for Action (2005) defines this term as the ability of an individual, an organization, or a country to learn from past disasters in organizing itself for disasters to reduce the same kind of risk in future events. However, according to the International Food Policy Research Institute (2013), resilience is the capability of physical infrastructure to properly absorb disaster shocks. Thus, disaster resilience could be considered the ability of the affected people to bounce back from shocks and adverse effects and improve their capacity to mitigate the impact of disasters.

Vulnerability

According to the IFRC (2016), vulnerability is the inability or weakened ability to foresee, to handle, to resist, or to recover from the impact of a threat. However, Cannon, Twigg, and Rowell (2016) note that it is not the same as poverty. Of course, being poor and being vulnerable in disasters are two different issues. Even the rich may be helpless in the face of disaster. According to Cannon, Twigg, and Rowell (2016), there is a close relationship between being poor and being troubled by natural disasters. The level of vulnerability relies on the type of livelihood of the community, and the agricultural population is more likely to be vulnerable in disaster situations.

Natural disasters create serious issues for agricultural sustainability. The rural farmers constantly contend with critical weather conditions, price variability of materials and harvests, livestock damages, and pest-related issues (Miranda and Vedenov 2001). The future activities of this community are fraught with uncertainty. On the other hand, banks and lenders hesitate to provide agricultural loans in view of the relatively high probability of default among farmers. Celia A. Harvey et al. (2014) urged the importance of taking adaptation measures to reduce the vulnerability of farmers during disasters.

Early Warning Systems

An early warning system can be identified as a key component of disaster risk reduction, which is important in preventing loss of lives and lowering the disasters' economic impact (*ISDR, 2006*). It is a technical device to predict possible disasters and related risks. According to ISDR (2006), early warning systems should have the following four components— (1) risk awareness, (2) monitoring and threatening service, (3) communication, and (4) response-ability. Thus, early warning systems facilitate public education and publicize warnings about risk.

Sustainable Agriculture

The term sustainable agriculture has received increased attention over the last three decades. Dictionaries define "sustain" as keeping in existence continuously or maintaining continuously with the implication of long-term support or permanence (http://www.yourdictionary.com, 2018). In developing countries, sustainable agriculture is identified as a critical factor for long-lasting and inclusive growth because of the cross-cutting nature of agriculture over all the other sectors (European Union 2012). With no agreed definition, sustainable agriculture has been defined from various perspectives. The European Union has identified four main reasons for introducing sustainable agricultural policies: (1) increasing demand for food under the pressure of the increasing population; (2) farming being a key weapon to combat poverty; (3) agriculture's twin role in adapting and mitigating climate change; and (4) the natural resource constraint in agriculture.

According to John Ikerd (quoted by Richard Duesterhaus 1990), sustainability pertains to agricultural and farming methods that are able to maintain their productivity and effectiveness to people indefinitely. Further, the authors note, such systems should have characteristics such as preserving resources, being socially helpful, economical, and environment friendly. Although their description relates to farming, the term sustainable can be better understood in a broader context in relation to social, economic, commercial, and environmental concern. Thus, sustainable agricultural policy concerns three main domains—economic, social, and environmental—and agricultural policies and strategies should be economically viable, socially fair, and environmentally sustainable.

D'Souza et al. (1993) discuss the specific practices that constitute a sustainable production system and classify a sustainable agricultural system as one that involves a combination of sustainable production practices. This study defines sustainable agriculture as one that links the use of several appropriate practices or technologies such as fertilizers, proper crop rotation, the use of combined pest control techniques, seedbed preparation, proper cultivation to control weeds, and control of the use of chemical-type products such as fertilizers, pesticides, growth stimulators, and various types of antibiotics. Thus, sustainable agriculture encourages the use of production practices that have the potential to reduce environmental damage.

Sustainable Agricultural Policies and Best Practices

The United Nations Report on Agriculture and Disaster (UN 2014) described risk reduction policies in developing countries and highlighted several areas that an agriculture-related national policy should focus on. These focal areas include agricultural planning, post disaster recovery assessment, agricultural legislation/policies, and capacities for disaster risk reduction in agricultural agencies, agricultural preparedness, annual budget allocation, agriculture-specific institutional mechanisms and setup. According to their framework, the following major areas are related to this study.

1. Prioritize critical sectors and themes, propose clear financial commitments, and reinforce the systematic incorporation to reduce disaster risk
2. Incorporate sectoral policies and plans with proper disaster risk reduction (DRR) mechanisms and climate change adaptation (CCA) strategies
3. Give priority to vulnerable groups in disaster situations
4. Integrate the humanitarian and developmental aspects of interventions for effective risk management in agriculture.

According to the United Nations Office for Disaster Risk Reduction (UNISDR) Cambodia has aligned its' agricultural policy with the guidelines given in Sendai Framework. The Cambodian Plan of Action for Disaster Risk Reduction in Agriculture (2013) has identified five key areas in its DRR plan.

1. Strong institutional and technical capacities with proper coordination mechanisms
2. Proactive DRR with early warning systems
3. Support for agricultural DRR through knowledge management and innovation
4. Reduction of vulnerabilities by implementing community-based programs
5. Inter-linkages of DRR and agricultural interventions.

These areas of focus are suitable for many DRR plans.

The success of any strategy, however, depends on the availability of related organizational arrangements, better coordination, and adequate resource allocations through government intervention.

The design of sustainable agricultural policies should incorporate various strategies to cope with vulnerability. The Nepal Government's Agricultural Policy (Nepal Law Commission 2014) highlighted several aspects for consideration in CCA and disaster risk management plans. Accordingly, the sustainable practices are:

1. Introduction of surveillance systems to assess the effect of disasters and mobilize relief schemes
2. Provision of special facilities to the targeted groups to construct and install small irrigation infrastructure
3. Development of safety nets (food and nutrition) for farmers when climate hazards and/or natural disasters occur
4. Extension of the existing livestock insurance programs
5. Minimization of the adverse impact of ecological issues in soil and water bodies resulting from use of agricultural chemicals.

Empirical Research on Sustainable Agricultural Practices

Celia A. Harvey et al. (2014) summarize the coping strategies resorted to by agricultural households when faced with challenges from disasters.

These strategies include giving up some of the daily meals, changing the regular menu, selling or mortgaging assets for food, borrowing money, borrowing food from neighbors or relatives, taking children out of school, sending them to work, sending adults to get outside jobs, renting their traditional lands to other people and/or receiving food aid from organizations. According to Celia A. Harvey et al. (2014), various strategies have been used by farmers in different disasters, and these are presented in Table 4.1.

Table 4.1 Various strategies used by farmers according to the nature of disasters

Disaster	Strategies used
Drought	• Change planting times • Use multiple crop varieties • Change crop sites or lands • Build a proper water-harvesting system for crops • Install home irrigation systems
Floods	• Replant crops after flooding subsides • Make diversion ditches to take water out of fields • Change crop planting times • Use multiple crop varieties • Stop farming land that was flooded
Climate changing situations	• Increase use of intercropping • Build a communal granary/food storage system to preserve crops • Shift field locations • Use diversified production systems by incorporating trees • Devise soil and water conservation practices • Use multiple crop varieties
Situation where water availability is changing due to climate change	• Use ditches to direct water/floods away from certain areas • Develop micro irrigation systems for crops • Build water-harvesting schemes for crops and livestock • Build water-harvesting system for domestic consumption

Source: Celia A. Harvey et al. (2014).

The State of New South Wales (1998) noted that in promoting the benefits of sustainable agriculture in society, all of the long-standing socioeconomic and environmental aspects are important. Weerakoon (2009) noted that sustainability prioritizes retention of soil fertility. In this regard, preservation of soil erosion, utilization of natural resources obtained from farmland or from the environment, such as cow dung, cow urine, leftovers from the previous farming season, waste materials, and plants are useful. Several sustainable agricultural practices adopted by Sri Lankan farmers have been summarized by the author and presented in Table 4.2.

Table 4.2 Sustainable agricultural practices adopted by Sri Lankan farmers

Agricultural practices	Examples of sustainable agricultural practices
Soil and water conservation	• Stone bunds and organic bunds • Eyebrow bunds • Mulching • SALT technology (Sloping Agricultural Land) • Alley cropping • Live fencing
Improving soil fertility	• Live compost pits • Wormy compost • Compost fertilizer • **Using straw as fertilizers**
Cropping systems	• Mixed cropping • Terracing • SRI System
Herbal pest control	• Neem mixture • Chili, Anoda (Annona muricata), garlic mixture • Leaf mixtures • Castor oil
Self-production of seeds	• Saving the balance seeds • Setting up plant nurseries • Selecting seeds and storing seeds

Source: Weerakoon L. (2009).

Policy Gaps, Analysis, and Methodologies

A policy gap is a difference between expected policy outcomes and observed policy outcomes. Identifying policy gaps is important because it can enhance policy performance (Dunn 2016). According to Dunn (2016), policy performance is the extent to which observed policy results contribute to solving the policy problem, and, in practice, policy performance is never perfect. Policy analysis is required in identifying policy gaps. Policy analysis refers to describing a policy from various perspectives (Fernando 2009). Policy analysis has been defined in various ways. Dunn (2016) defines policy analysis as a process of multidisciplinary inquiry aiming at the creation of critical assessment and communication of policy-relevant information. Various methods could be used to analyze a policy, and they all involve different kinds of judgments (Dunn 2016). The policy analysis methodology is not limited to any specific social science field (Dunn 2016), but is methodologically eclectic, allowing practitioners to freely select a method from among scientific methods, whether qualitative or quantitative, as long as it produces reliable information.

To analyze the policy gaps, Dunn (2016) proposed four methods, as mentioned in Table 4.3.

Table 4.3 Methods of policy analysis

Method	Description
Prospective and retrospective analysis	Prospective analysis seeks to transform information before policy actions are taken, whereas retrospective analysis is an ex-post analysis (done after the policies have been implemented). This ex-post analysis is normally of three kinds: 1. Discipline-oriented approach - tries to advance and experiment with discipline-based theories that describe the roots and consequences of policies. 2. Problem-oriented approach - seeks to explain practical problems in implementing policies. 3. Application-oriented approach - seeks to explain the causes and consequences of policies in relation to their goals and objectives.
Descriptive analysis and normative analysis	This method tries to explain, comprehend, and foresee the policies by understanding patterns of causality, whereas normative analysis tries to provide prescriptions on policy performance and desired policies.
Problem-finding and problem-solving analysis	In this method, problem-finding analysis seeks to discover problems of policy definition, whereas problem-solving analysis seeks to solve problems rather than find them.
Segmented and integrated analysis	This method seeks to bridge several pillars of multidisciplinary policy analysis.

Source: Dunn 2016.

According to Hogwood and Gunn (1984), policy can be analyzed in terms of its content, process, output, evaluation, information study, process advocacy, and policy advocacy, and its analysis can be either prescriptive or descriptive.

Data Analysis and Discussion

This section consists of two main parts. The first part of this section summarizes the existing agricultural policy in Sri Lanka in terms of its policy statement, goals and objectives, and existing institutional mechanism; the second part examines the strengths and weaknesses of agricultural policy in Sri Lanka.

Analysis of Agricultural Policy in Sri Lanka

According to the National Agriculture Policy of the Ministry of Agricultural Development and Agrarian Services in Sri Lanka, the present agricultural policy focuses on major goals and objectives, namely (1) Increasing domestic agricultural production to ensure food and nutrition security of the nation, (2) Enhancing agricultural productivity to ensure sustainable growth, (3) Maximizing benefits and minimizing adverse effects of globalization on agriculture, both domestic and export-oriented, (4) Adopting productive farming systems and improved agro-technologies with a view to reducing the unit cost of production and increasing profit, (5) Adopting farming technologies that are environment friendly and harmless to health, (6) Promoting agro-based industries and increasing employment opportunities, and (7) Enhancing the income and living standards of the farming community.

The National Agriculture Policy (2015) includes a policy statement that directs several important aspects of the policy, some of whose salient features are as follows:

Promoting Agricultural Production
The policy focuses on ensuring that agricultural production in the country is technically sound and economically viable. It promotes environmentally sound and socially acceptable programs aimed at achieving sustainable agricultural growth and proper utilization of resources.

Seeds and Planting Materials

The policy aims to produce and supply high-quality seeds to farmers. This also involves planting materials of commercial varieties in a viable environment focusing on both state and private sector participation.

Fertilizers

The policy discourages the use of chemical fertilizers and promotes the production and utilization of organic and bio-fertilizers in agricultural production, with the ultimate aim of reducing the use of chemical fertilizers through Integrated Plant Nutrition Systems (IPNS).

Pesticides

The policy encourages minimization of the use of synthetic pesticides in agriculture all activities and promotes bio pesticides and Integrated Pest Management (IPM) in the production process.

Irrigation and Water Management

The policy encourages the use of efficient water management and moisture retention techniques in achieving high productivity in agriculture. It helps to conserve the existing water resources for sustainable agricultural development.

Agricultural Credit

The policy aims to strengthen rural credit institutions in the country, which are connected with farmers' investments, savings, and risk management activities. It also envisages simplified procedures for providing loans for agricultural activities.

Postharvest Technology

The policy promotes and develops better harvesting and processing techniques for farmers to increase the value addition of agricultural production. Further, the policy aims to develop storage and transport methods to minimize pre- and postharvest losses and thereby improve the quality of production to meet domestic and export market demands.

Institutional Mechanism of Agricultural Policy in Sri Lanka

Several organizations are responsible for the implementation of the policy.

Ministry of Agriculture in Sri Lanka

Ministry of agriculture is the main authority responsible for all agriculture-related activities in Sri Lanka. Currently, several organizations and departments are operating under the ministry.

1. Department of Agriculture

   The objectives of the Department of Agriculture are to maintain and increase productivity and production of the food crop and enhance the income and living conditions of the farmers. The department is involved in making food available at affordable prices to the consumer. Its major functions include research, extension, production of seed and planting material, and regulatory services related to plant quarantine, soil conservation, and pesticides (Department of Agriculture 2016).

2. Department of Agrarian Development

   The mission of the department is the formulation and timely implementation of institutional facilitator, legal and management services for optimum productivity of all agriculture lands as well as the sustainable development of the farming community. The department is involved in various tasks in agrarian development to ensure the maximum utilization of agricultural lands in accordance with the government's agricultural policies. This department makes arrangements to protect the cultivation rights of agricultural landlords and occupiers/tenant cultivators, making regulations regarding registration and functioning of farmers' organizations (Department of Agrarian Development 2013).

Agricultural and Agrarian Insurance Board

The agricultural and agrarian insurance board provides insurance services for agriculture-related activities in Sri Lanka. Currently, it provides agricultural crop insurance, livestock insurance, tractors and agricultural machinery insurance, store insurance, health care insurance, and accident insurance (Agricultural Insurance Board 2016).

1. Agricultural Crop Insurance

   The agricultural and agrarian insurance board is currently providing paddy, buckwheat crop, vegetable crop, and other crop insurance for farmers (Agricultural Insurance Board 2016).

2. Livestock Insurance

   The aim of this insurance is to reduce the risk of farmers engaged in the livestock industry, improve dairy production, and encourage the younger population of the industry by providing a fixed survival pattern. The main focus of this policy is on cattle and goats because they are the most common livestock in Sri Lanka (Agricultural Insurance Board 2016).

3. Tractors and Agricultural Machinery Insurance

   The main aim of this insurance is to provide coverage for devices such as tractors used by those engaged in agriculture and also for agricultural equipment such as water pumps and leaf harvester machines. Investors will be encouraged into mechanization in agriculture (Agricultural Insurance Board 2016).

4. Storage Insurance

   This insurance scheme has been introduced to minimize the risk of investors' assembled stocks and is designed to provide insurance coverage to cover the cost of damage in natural disasters as well as that caused by animals and insects to stocks (Agricultural Insurance Board 2016)

5. Healthcare Insurance

   The aim of this insurance scheme is to reduce the financial difficulties faced by hospitalization of farmers due to accidents or illness (Agricultural Insurance Board 2016).

6. Accident Insurance

   This insurance covers accidents involving farmers, and bereaved family members would find the insurance plan helpful (Agricultural Insurance Board 2016).

Hector Kobbekaduwa Agrarian Research and Training Institute (HKATI)

The role of this organization is mainly to generate a range of policy analyses that cover key aspects of human and resource development in the agrarian sector. It has developed into a premier national institute in the field of socioeconomic research involving the use of land and water. It has also developed the necessary skills and infrastructure for providing relevant training to farmers, field workers, and managers in both the state and the nonstate sectors (Hector Kobbekaduwa Agrarian Research and Training Institute 2014).

Sri Lanka Council for Agricultural Research Policy

This is to ensure that agricultural research, development, and innovations are directed toward national development goals through policy formulation, facilitation, coordination, monitoring and evaluation, and impact assessment and published in journals (Sri Lanka Council for Agricultural Research Policy 2016).

Institute of Postharvest Technology

This institute functions under the Ministry of Agriculture Development and Agrarian Services. It is the main institution in Sri Lanka engaged in improving the postharvest technology of rice/other grains, field crops, fruits and vegetables, and spices through research, training and extension, consultancy, advisory, and other development activities (The Institute of Post Harvest Technology 2016).

National Food Promotion Board

The main objectives of this board are:

1. To provide incentives to develop the economic and social status of the agricultural community and guide them in achieving a sustainable agricultural pattern;
2. To make strategic recommendations and safeguard their coordination for organizations involved in local agricultural activities;
3. To coordinate and secure the aid of local and foreign agencies for the Government's agricultural programs;
4. To monitor and provide recommendations to local and foreign nongovernmental organizations engaged in agriculture;
5. To act as a party intervenient to encourage and coordinate technical and other aids of agricultural investment;

6. To provide incentives for agricultural product diversification, increasing productivity and product distribution and marketing;

7. To take suitable technology to the agricultural community for yield management, value addition for products and packaging; and

8. To provide incentives to the community to promote the usage and awareness of indigenous and traditional agricultural crops (Sri Lanka National Freedom from Hunger Campaign Board 2011).

Ceylon Fertilizer Company Ltd

The company is making sustained efforts to promote agricultural development in Sri Lanka by supplying quality products to the agricultural sector via the marketing infrastructure and support network of warehouses all over the country (Ceylon Fertilizer Company Ltd 2015).

Strengths and Weaknesses of Sri Lankan Agricultural Policy

The agricultural policy in Sri Lanka has some strengths in terms of sustainable considerations. The policy consists of multiple goals and objectives to promote agriculture with a view to achieving risk reduction in disasters. The focal areas of the agricultural policy are an increase in agricultural production, reduction of farming cost, promotion of agro-based industries, and improvement of employment opportunities for farmers. Several steps have been taken to establish an institutional mechanism to meet these goals.

Encouraging the development of water control and water conservation techniques is one of the areas of concern for DRR in the sustainable agricultural policy. The agricultural policy in Sri Lanka incorporates this aspect in its policy statement under irrigation and water management. Under the irrigation and water management section of the policy, consideration was given to (a) protection of irrigation reservoirs, canals, drainage systems, and other structures from damage by climate; (b) usage and stimulating conservation of rainwater and groundwater;

and (c) increasing water use efficiency and promoting modern and intensive irrigation technologies for water conservation. However, the effectiveness of all the organizational initiatives needs to be assessed using empirical data.

In regard to agricultural credit and insurance, the policy encourages the strengthening of rural credit institutions connected with farmers' investments, saving, and risk management. Thus, the initiation of appropriate agricultural insurance schemes helps farmers to reduce risk associated with natural calamities. However, informal discussions with several farmers disclosed a gap between the current level of external supports and farmers' capability to adapt to climate change. Hence, the government's intervention seems inadequate to coping properly with climate changes.

The policy documents have several notable weaknesses in their avowed aim of promoting sustainable agriculture with a view to achieving risk reduction during disasters. These weaknesses may be highlighted as follows.

Even though the concept of sustainable agriculture integrates the three main goals of environmental health, economic profitability, and social and economic equity, the existing policy focuses solely on improving productivity. Measures to ensure social justice, as well as environmental sustainability, seem inadequate. As the farmers' main source of subsistence is agriculture, their income levels are very low. That situation violates the principle of social and economic justice. Besides, no attempt has been made to promote diversification of agriculture and diversification of the livelihood of the farmers, and farmers have, as a result, become more vulnerable, both economically and socially.

Environmental sustainability means protecting the natural environment for the future generations while engaging in agriculture to achieve the needs of the present generation. This is another dimension of sustainable agriculture. Under the agricultural policy, no organization has taken the responsibility of preserving the environment. Even though the policy statement emphasizes the promotion, production, and utilization of organic and bio-fertilizers in agricultural activities, no serious attempt has been made to realize that goal. Even though the Ceylon

Fertilizer Corporation LTD has functioned for the last 50 years under the Ministry of Agriculture, its main mission is "ensuring the profitable sustainability of the company by manufacturing and distributing fertilizer catering to the multitude of market demands in order to increase products, income, and profitability in the Sri Lanka agricultural and Farmer Community services with the maximum contribution of the 'Lakeshore family' in compliance with state policies" (The Ceylon Fertilizer Corporation LTD 2017). Hence, the company seems to promote the use of chemical fertilizers, which have to be imported. The use of chemical fertilizer is recognized as one of the main causes of water pollution, deterioration of farmers' health (kidney disease), and soil degradation. The promotion of sustainable agriculture, however, requires that the use of organic fertilizer be encouraged, yet it has received inadequate attention.

Promoting and enhancing early warning systems in the interest of proactive DRR and climate change adoption is a major element in the effort to ensure sustainable agriculture. However, the policy pays no attention to the need to establish the improved use of climate and weather information and forecasts or of early warning systems about potential disasters, leaving farmers vulnerable to disasters.

Even though several institutions are involved in agricultural research and are mainly responsible for national policy formulation and implementation, no authorities are effectively responsible for improving awareness among farmers and for introducing appropriate crop selection, cultivation methods, and new varieties of crops, quick-growing crops, and alternative farming systems to sustain them and create resilience in disaster situations. This too leaves farmers vulnerable to disasters.

There appears to be no awareness among farmers of livelihood diversification practices and of good practices for DRR to increase the resilience of existing farming systems and appropriate methods of land and natural resources. Despite the range of institutions under the Ministry of Agriculture involved in research and training relevant to agriculture, every organization performs its role in isolation with no proper coordination.

Thus, although there are various organizations implementing programs aimed at sustainable agriculture, the effectiveness of these programs is yet to be established.

Recommendations

In light of the weaknesses of the policies, the following suggestions are proposed to enhance and maintain a sustainable agricultural policy in the country.

Enhance Public Awareness about Disaster-Prone Lands and Time Periods

The authorities concerned should take measures to increase public awareness about disaster-prone areas, particularly residential and agricultural lands. After the Geographical Survey and Mines Bureau has properly identified particular areas as disaster-prone land, the government should classify them as such by prohibiting human settlements or agriculture. This strategy has been followed in Uganda and in New South Wales and should be considered in Sri Lanka because people hardly have access to those documents, such as the government's gazettes (the authorized document that publishes the government's special news, decisions, and job vacancies), especially at the village level. Thus, the local authority would do well to display some danger or early warning notices about potential disasters. This would enhance public awareness about the disaster-prone lands and get them to relocate.

Provide Proper Consultation for Farmers on Strategies for Resilient Agriculture

Farmers are the most vulnerable and immediately affected group in a disaster and hence should be well informed about prearrangements for disasters to reduce the adverse impact on agriculture. Hence, the authorities concerned could provide them with occasional consultations on how to reduce disaster risk. For example, farmers could be instructed about the appropriate crop selection for different climatic situations. They could also be informed about crop varieties, fast-growing corps, need for changing locations, timing of crop planting, and new cultivation methods. In particular, contingency crop planning (such as intercrop farming) and post harvesting techniques should be introduced to make the agricultural sector sustainable. Similar strategies are found in Madagascar, where a study was conducted by Harvey et al. (2014) on the extreme vulnerability of smallholder farmers to climate change and agricultural risk.

Introduce Livelihood Diversification Practices to Vulnerable Communities

Farmers in most cases live in a vicious cycle of poverty owing to regular shocks, low yield, low income, increased debt burden, and so on. As proneness to disaster risk is inevitable in any country, farmers' livelihood activities need to be diversified and alternate employment opportunities provided. For example, some countries, such as Nepal and Bhutan, have introduced "agro tourism," providing an additional source of income for farmers.

Preserve and Reawaken Indigenous Agricultural Knowledge and Technology

Sri Lanka possessed excellent eco-friendly agricultural technology and knowledge in the past. Considerable evidence is still found on sustainable agricultural practices in early Sri Lankan history. Farmers had sound indigenous agricultural knowledge that was robust even in disasters. Unfortunately, that implicit knowledge and agricultural technology used by the early farmers has deteriorated since the introduction of the plantation sector by the Europeans. However, the authorities concerned should act swiftly to revive and preserve the country's traditional, indigenous agricultural knowledge in ensuring sustainability in this field.

Increased Access to Credit and Safety Nets

During disasters and following catastrophic events, such as those pre-cipitated by extreme weather, many farmers depend on informal sup-port gained from relations or acquaintances. As many formal safety nets are inaccessible to farmers or not immediately operational, farmers af-fected by disasters become more vulnerable and struggle to survive. It is therefore necessary to establish formal and working safety nets and also strengthen existing mechanisms such as the agricultural insurance scheme.

Encourage Farmers to Use Organic Fertilizers

To establish a system of sustainable agriculture calls for significantly in-creased compliance with eco-friendly practices and techniques. Because of the poor uptake in this field, farmers in the North Central province currently suffer from serious kidney issues as well. It is therefore neces-sary to encourage the use of sustainable agricultural practices and mate-rials (such as fertilizers and pesticides), by promoting the use of organic fertilizers (as they are healthy and eco-friendly) and discouraging the use of chemical pesticides (as they damage species living in the soil and water).

Establish Proper Coordination among Agricultural Institutions

There are a plethora of agencies in the field of agriculture, but it is ques-tionable whether they are sufficiently well coordinated. No institution, therefore, takes immediate and direct responsibility for anything that happens. Especially in times of disaster, the agricultural sector and the farmers are severely affected, and the media is abuzz with reports from farmers who complain about the unsatisfactory support provided by these institutions. Further, without proper coordination, public resources are wasted by the authorities through duplication of activities. Hence, proper coordination among the institutions is necessary for a sustainable agricul-ture policy.

Recognize Disaster Resilience as a Key Priority Area in Agriculture

Even though a comprehensive institutional mechanism for the agricultural sector exists in Sri Lanka, no institution makes disaster resilience one of its priorities. All the institutions have a separate set of functions and responsibilities and do not function beyond that scope. Currently, the government takes several ad hoc actions to make the community resilient when a disaster occurs, but no proper mechanism has been established. In light of all that has been discussed and recommended, it is essential that measures be taken toward disaster resilience, and thus the direct responsibility should be allocated to a separate or existing institution, as only then would such an institution perform and advance in this area.

Conclusion

Sri Lanka is a developing country with a comparatively large rural agricultural sector. Floods, earthquakes, and droughts are its most common natural disasters. People involved in the agriculture sector are the rural poor, who are adversely and frequently affected by natural disasters. The country's agriculture policy does not adequately address, the adverse effects on agriculture due to disasters. This study has examined the strengths and weaknesses of the existing agricultural policy in the light of the concept of sustainable agriculture. The strengths of the existing policy are its emphasis on encouragement of the development of water control and water conservation techniques, agricultural credit and insurance, and strengthening of rural credit systems. However, these programs need remedial attention in the following areas: establishing the improved use of climate and weather information and forecasts; early warning about potential disasters; improving farmers' awareness and introducing appropriate crop selection; cultivation methods; and new varieties of crops and quick-growing crops to sustain themselves in disasters.

The analysis has identified best practices used in other countries to strengthen the policy, recommending the following steps as a means toward this end: to enhance public awareness about disaster-prone lands and time periods, to instruct farmers on strategies for achieving agricultural resilience, to ensure proper coordination among agricultural institutions, to recognize disaster resilience as a key priority in the agricultural sector, and to encourage the use of organic fertilizers. These recommendations will be a useful input in the creation of future policy on sustainable agriculture in Sri Lanka.

Limitations of the Study

The study is based mainly on secondary data, and this constitutes one of its limitations. Further, studies should be conducted to assess organizational effectiveness on the basis of primary data, obtained from farmers and relevant agricultural institutions.

References

Action for Disaster Risk Reduction in Agriculture. 2013. 2014–2018, Sri Lanka National Agriculture Policy. 2015. http://www.agrimin.gov.lk/web/index.php/en/downloads/policy

Agricultural & Agrarian Insurance Board. 2016. http://www.aib.gov.lk/insurence_schemes.html (accessed October 23, 2016).

Cannon, T., T. Twigg, and J. Rowell. 2016. *Social Vulnerability, Sustainable Livelihood and Disasters*. London, UK: Sustainable Livelihood Support Office.

Central Bank of Sri Lanka (CBSL). 2016. Annual Report Chapter One. pp. 168–70.

Ceylon Fertilizer Company Ltd. February, 2015. Overview. http://www.lakpohora.lk/web/index.php?option=com_content&view=article&id=46&Itemid=53&lang=en (accessed October 22, 2016).

Department of Agrarian Development, Ministry of Agriculture. 2013. Performance Report 2013. p. 86.

Disaster Management Information System in Sri Lanka. 2016. *Recent Disasters: Disaster Information Management System in Sri Lanka.* http://www.desinventar.lk (accessed October 24, 2016).

D'Souza, G., and D. Cyphers, and T. Phipps. October, 1993. "Factors Affecting the Adoption of Sustainable Agricultural Practices." *Agricultural and Resource Economics Review* 22, pp. 159–65.

Dunn, W.M. 2016. *Public Policy Analysis*. 5th ed. London & New York, UK: Routledge.

European Union. 2012. *A Strategic Approach to EU Agricultural Research & Innovation*. European Union.

Fernando, R.L.S. 2009. *Public Policy Analysis*. Nugegoda, Sri Lanka: Deepani Printers Ltd Company.

Food and Agriculture Organization of the United Nation. 2015. *A Call for Action to Build Resilient Livelihoods*. http://www.fao.org

Harvey, C. A., Z. L. Rakotobe, N. S. Rao, R. Dave, H. Razafimahatratra, R. H. Rabarijohn, H. Rajaofara, and J. L. MacKinnon. April 5, 2014. "Extreme Vulnerability of Smallholder Farmers to Agricultural Risks and Climate Change in Madagascar." *Philosophical Transactions of the Royal Society B: Biological Sciences* 369, no. 1639, p. 20130089.

Hogwood, B. W., and L. A. Gunn. 1984. *Policy Analysis for the Real World*. Oxford, UK: Oxford University Press.

International Strategy for Disaster Risk Reduction. 2006. "Developing Early Warning Systems." Third International Conference on Early Warning: March 2006, Bonn, Germany.

International Water Management Institute. 2014. *Solutions for a Water-secure World, Strategy 2014-2018*. http://www.iwmi.cgiar.org/About_IWMI/PDF/iwmi-strategy-2014-2018.pdf

Kobbekaduwa Agrarian Research and Training Institute. 2014. *Home Page*. http://www.harti.gov.lk/index.php/en (accessed October 24, 2016).

Miranda, M.J., and D.V. Vedenov. 2001. "Rainfall Insurance for Midwest Crop Production." Columbus, OH: Department of AED Economics.

Nepal Law Commission, Nepal. 2014. *National Agricultural Policy*. http://www.lawcommission.gov.np (accessed July 7, 2016).

Plan of Action for Disaster Risk Reduction in Agriculture. 2013. 2014–2018, Sri Lanka National Agriculture Policy. 2015. http://www.agrimin.gov.lk/web/index.php/en/downloads/policy

Sri Lanka Council for Agricultural Research Policy. 2016. Directory. http://link2srilanka.com/business-directory/1875/welcome-carp-home-page (accessed October 17, 2016).

Sri Lanka Council for Agricultural Research Policy. 2016. Directory. http://link2srilanka.com/business-directory/1875/welcome-carp-home-page (accessed October 17, 2016).

Sri Lanka National Freedom from Hunger Campaign Board. 2011. Annual Report.http://www.parliament.lk/uploads/documents/paperspresented/annual-report-srilanka-national-freedom-from-hunger-campaign-board-2014.pdf

The Department of Agriculture. 2016. About Us. http://www.doa.gov.lk/index.php/en/ct-menu-item-3 (accessed October 24, 2016).

The Institute of Post Harvest Technology. 2016. Overview. http://ipht.lk/About%20us/Overview.html (accessed October 23, 2016).

The International Federation of Red Cross and Red Crescent Societies. 2016. http://www.ifrc.org (accessed October, 2016).

The International Food Policy Research Institute. 2013. http://www.ifpri.org (accessed October, 2016).

United Nations Office for the Coordination of Humanitarian Affairs. 2014. *Humanitarian Bulletin.* https://reliefweb.int/sites/reliefweb.int/files/resources/Humanitarian%20Bulletin_SRI%20LANKA_Aug%202014.pdf

UNISDR. 2005. "Hyogo Framework for Action 2005-2015: Building the Resilience of Nations and Communities to Disasters." World Conference on Disaster Reduction, 18–22 January 2005, Kobe, Hyogo, Japan.

UN Office for Disaster Risk Reduction (UNISDR). 2013. *Disaster Risk Reduction in the United Nations.* https://www.unisdr.org/files/32918_drrintheun2013.pdf

UN World Conference on Disaster Risk Reduction (WCDRR). 2015. Agriculture and Disaster Risk, https://www.wcdrr.org/documents/wcdrr/prepcom1/UN/ATTFONWO.pdf. retrieved on 3 December 2018.

Weerakon L. 2009. *Sustainable Agriculture Policy and Development Programme in Sri Lanka, Movement for National Land and Agricultural Reform.* Sri Lanka: Centre for Sustainable Agriculture Research and Development.

World Bank. 2016. "Agriculture Value Added % of GDP." https://data.worldbank.org/indicator/NV.AGR.TOTL.ZS (accessed June 2018).

World Bank. June, 2017a. *Employment in Agriculture.* https://data.world-bank.org/indicator/SL.AGR.EMPL.ZS?name_desc=falseWhatis .techtarget.com (accessed August 05, 2018).

World Bank. 2017b. *World Development Indicators, Structure of output.* http://wdi.worldbank.org/table/4.2

CHAPTER 5

Natural Disasters and Agriculture in Bangladesh: Planning and Management

Nasim Banu

Department of Development Studies, Islamic University,
Kushtia, Bangladesh

Introduction

Bangladesh is a country with a population of 166 million people, in a geographic area of 144,000 sq. km. Here, people depend mostly on agriculture for their livelihood. Agriculture is an integrated activity with an interrelationship between crops and noncrops like livestock, fishery, and forestry. Crops and noncrops of agriculture are equally vulnerable and at risk of natural disasters arising from intensified global climate change. Agriculture is the mainstay of Bangladesh, as reflected in its share in the gross domestic product (GDP) and employment. During the sixth five-year plan (FYP) period (2011–2015), the agricultural sector achieved a GDP growth of 3.5 percent against average GDP growth of 6.3 percent. The agricultural sector employs 47.5 percent of the labor force and accounts for about 5 percent of the total export earnings of Bangladesh (GoB 2015). Bangladesh's soil is alluvial and fertile; sufficient water is available during the monsoon, which supports agricultural production in the country throughout the year. Heavy rainfall during the monsoon and the three mighty rivers, namely, the Ganges, Brahmaputra, and Meghna, with networks of more than 200 streams and tributaries, are the main source of water for agriculture, though Bangladesh has very little control over its water resources as it enters from the upper riparian country. Heavy rainfall in the monsoons and extreme water flow in rivers is the main cause of natural disasters in the form of floods and river erosion. In addition, the coastal zone of the country frequently suffers water-related hazards owing to cyclones with tidal surges, which are the cause of salinity intrusion. During the period 2006 to 2011, Bangladesh experienced aggregate losses of US$114 million from eleven floods and US$2,570 million from fifteen cyclones and most of these losses were in agriculture. Thus, finding a solution to address the threat of natural disasters for agricultural production has been a national objective of the planning of the government of Bangladesh (GoB), to ensure that resources used and operations launched to counter disaster produce the best possible results.

Research Objectives

The core objectives of this chapter are: (i) to identify the natural disasters that most hamper the growth of agricultural production in Bangladesh; and (ii) to evaluate the planning and programs necessary to prevent agricultural loss caused by natural disasters and maintain the food security and environmental sustainability of the country.

The broad objectives are based mainly on the following research questions:

I. What are the natural disasters and what are the main causes of their occurrences that mostly affect the agricultural production in Bangladesh?

II. How much damage occurred to agricultural production because of the recent natural disasters?

III. How do the public planning and programs envisage protecting agricultural production from natural disaster?

This chapter attempts to find answers to these questions and makes recommendations aimed at promoting sustainable growth of agricultural production in Bangladesh.

Methodology

The chapter focuses on the impact of natural disasters on agricultural production and the government strategies and programs to protect agricultural production to ensure food security for the people and development of the nation. Comprehensive desk-based research has been done on the basis of historical data from previous occurrences. Selected occurrences of natural disasters were evaluated, and the necessary data was collected from government reports and documents on planning and programs undertaken. Moreover, data pertaining to the impact of various natural disasters on agriculture in Bangladesh as well as the evaluation of governmental initiatives and programs designed to protect agricultural production from natural disasters has helped to form the theoretical basis of this chapter.

Natural Disasters and Agricultural Production

Bangladesh is a low-lying delta with several rivers and their tributaries (Rawlani and Sovacool 2011). The country's environment is under threat from natural disasters that include floods, river erosion, drought, cyclones, accompanied by storm surges and salinity ingress, in the coastal belt, mostly because of its geographical location, monsoon, and the impact of global climate change. The intensification of the global climate change aggravates the risk to Bangladesh from these threats, which adversely impact both human and natural systems. Human systems include rivers, water bodies, agriculture, and so on; natural systems include rainfall, mangroves, tropical forests, ecosystem, and so on. Natural disasters are becoming more frequent and devastating in terms of economic losses and human casualties in Bangladesh, owing to its geographical location, global warming, and climate change associated with its high density of population. Natural disasters destroy infrastructure, property, agricultural assets (crops, livestock, fishery, and forestry), and economic activities, and thus poverty prevails. However, only the types of natural disasters that most affect agricultural production will be discussed here.

Floods

Bangladesh experiences twin problems relating to water i.e. excess during the rainy season and scarcity during the dry period. Excessive rainfall, causing a threat of floods, poses a serious risk to agricultural production, while drought affects the overall availability of water for crops and non-crop production. Floods are a regular occurrence in Bangladesh, affecting 30 to 50 percent of the total land surface (GoB 2011). They result from heavy rainfall in the monsoon season, drainage congestion, high tides/storm surges, and overflowing of major rivers with high water levels coming from upstream. Normal river flooding regularly affects 20 percent of the country, and up to 68 percent in extreme cases (GoB 2010a, b). Normal flooding provides the soil with vital moisture and fertility, and is hence considered a blessing for crop production. However, floods can also inundate large areas of the country, causing massive destruction to agriculture and deaths of people and livestock, homelessness, and damage to homes and infrastructure. They also cause riverbank erosion; thus, when erosion results from widespread floods, the destruction becomes colossal, with loss of standing crops and cultivable land.

There are four types of floods in Bangladesh.

I. Flash floods—encountered in the northern and eastern parts of the country during April to May and September to November;
II. Rain floods—triggered by heavy rains and drainage congestion;
III. Monsoon floods—caused by monsoon rains, affecting major rivers from mid-August to mid-October;
IV. Coastal floods—caused by storm surges and tides (Azad, Hossain, and Nasreen 2013).

Primary causes of floods in Bangladesh are heavy rainfall during monsoons; snow melting in the Himalayas during August to September; deposits of sediment in riverbeds; causing drainage congestion; deforestation in the catchment area; unplanned construction of roads and embankments; depressions in the Bay of Bengal; and magnitude of the winds, and construction of barrages in rivers by the riparian country. During the flooding period, a majority of the agriculture-based households suffer standing crop losses, and women and marginal land owners mostly lose their homesteads along with their vegetable, livestock, and poultry production. These landless households are thus rendered unemployed.

Bangladesh witnessed extreme floods in 1974, 1987, and 1988, and regular floods in 2004 and 2007, as shown in Table-5.1. Two consecutive floods occurred in 1988 that lasted for 65 days.

Table 5.1 Areas inundated and losses on account of major floods

Flood		1974	1987	1988	1988	2004	2007
Affected area (%)	40		30	60	67	38	42
Economic loss (US$ in billion)	Crop production lowered by 15%		1.0	1.2	2.8	6.6	2.2

Source: GoB (2010a, b).

Bangladesh was affected most by the floods of 2017, when about 700,000 homes were partially or totally destroyed (George 2017). The floods of 1984 caused seasonal losses of paddy production of about 1 million Mt and employment reduction of 25 million-person days. In 2000, the country faced an unusual flood in its hitherto flood-free southwestern region that resulted in massive damage to agriculture and infrastructure.

Apart from the losses shown in Table 5.2, one of the country's most severe pre-monsoon and monsoon floods occurred in 2017, affecting more than 8 million people in 32 districts, that is, in more than one-third of the country's territory, killing 145 people and damaging 620,000 homes. Hence, the GoB had to prepare an initial emergency response plan, at a cost of US$12 million, to provide food, shelter, and harvesting materials. The pre-monsoon floods of 2017 submerged vast swathes of land, destroying rice production on about 362,000 hectares, including areas that were nearly ready for harvest on about 160,170 hectares in the Hoar area, the northeast region of the country. Heavy rainfall as well as onrush of water from the upstream led to the inundation of vast areas of croplands of Hoar and the low-lying northeast region.

The northern part of the country also faced monsoon floods in 2017 (mid-July to mid-August), caused by excessive monsoon rainfall and upstream water flow, that caused water logging and difficulties for the population of the affected area and damaged crops. These floods destroyed standing crops, mostly rice, and delayed the next crop cycle by at least two months in nine northern districts, which were the worst affected by the calamity. Also damaged were vegetable crops on 3,317 hectares and the Aman crop on 201,000 hectares.

Table 5.2 Losses on account of Hoar floods in 2017

Destroyed area of rice production	Loss of rice production	Loss of local farmers' day labor	Damaged potential rice crop	Loss due to damaged rice crop (US$)
160,170 hectare	800,000 Mt	192,204,000 person day	354,840 Mt	10,645.2 million

Source: *The Daily Star* (2017a), *The Daily Star* (2017b), *Dhaka Tribune* (2017), *The Independent* (2017).

Flooding is also the major cause of riverbank erosion, which is quite high during the starting and receding times of a flood, The magnitude of destruction in this case is enormous, and 10,000 hectares of land is eroded every year (GoB 2001). A study shows that during the period 1973 to 2004, riverbank erosion along the Padma and Jamuna rivers was 29,390 and 87,790 hectors of land, respectively. The eroded land was mostly agricultural land.

Drought

Drought creates the condition of having a lack of water to meet the normal needs of agriculture, livestock, and people and is generally associated with semiarid or desert climates. Drought is an unpredictable natural hazard that affects seasonal crops, fruit-bearing trees, forestry, and the environment in Bangladesh. Water shortage is mainly due to the continual absence of rainfall or low rainfall, leading to the reduction of stream flow, groundwater, soil moisture, and desertification in those parts of the country that are severely affected. In the context of Bangladesh, drought can be defined as dry soil condition for a period when the soil moisture supply is less than what is required for satisfactory crop production (Brammer 2007). The northern region of Bangladesh suffers the most through the loss of as much as 17 percent of rice production (see Table 5.3) (GoB 2010a,b) and, based on the severity of the drought, crop losses can range between 20 percent and 60 percent. Drought is a temporary, spatially irregular, and nonperiodic phenomenon, which reduces crop production, and farmers' incomes, drastically.

Table 5.3 The severe drought years in Bangladesh

Year of drought	Affected area (%)	Reduced rice production (Mt)
1972	42.48	—
1979	42.04	2.0 million
1995	40.00	3.5 million

Source: GoB (2010a, b).

Cyclones and Storm Surges

Cyclones associated with storm surges cause catastrophic devastation to life, agriculture, mangrove forests, and properties of Bangladesh. From independence, in 1971, till 2009, Bangladesh witnessed the occurrence of eleven cyclones, along with related storm surges, that destroyed agricultural assets, including forests, damaged embankments and other infrastructure, and killed more than 168,000 people. Victims lost all their possessions, including standing crops, and the Sundarbans mangrove forest was destroyed. Hence, marginal and landless people lost their employment opportunities and livelihoods and had to migrate elsewhere to find jobs to survive (Table- 5.4). The cyclone "Aila" alone caused damage to agriculture estimated at US$155.3 million.

Saline Water Intrusion

Salinity intrusion is primarily a seasonal phenomenon in Bangladesh that affects the coastal region of the country; the affected area rises from 10 percent in the monsoon to over 40 percent in the dry season (GoB 2010a, b). Agricultural production (including fisheries and livestock) and the Sundarbans mangrove forest are affected by salinity, particularly

Table 5.4 Damage and loss due to devastating cyclone in Bangladesh

Events	Cyclone Bhola (1970)	Cyclone Gorkey (1995)	Cyclone Sidr (2007)	Cyclone Aila (2009)
Area affected	12%	11%	48%	12.5%
Crops damaged	1.2 million acres	0.35 million acres	2.4 million acres	95,920 acres
Livestock lost	—	—	1,778,507	62,472
Homes damaged	85%	1,000,000	2,300,000	181,028
People homeless	3,600,000	10,000,000	1,522,077	637,851
Loss of life	400,000			

Source: Banu (2015).

in the dry season. High salinity in the monsoon and dry seasons in the southwest part of the country is associated with a decrease in the flow of upstream freshwater as well as silting of major river channels. The upstream diversion of the Ganges has resulted in the increase in salinity downstream which has affected more than 10,000 square miles, causing manifold problems such as crop damage, river water turning impotable, increased incidence of waterborne diseases, and disruption of industrial operations in the Khulna industrial belt (Ali, Islam, and Kuddus 1996). About 1.2 million hectares of arable land are affected by direct salinity intrusion, which is expected to increase in the future (GoB 2011). However, owing to the inundation by sea water and saline water intrusion, the land for crop farming along the large coastal belt of Bangladesh is reducing gradually.

Planning and Management Related to Natural Disasters

Agriculture is still the mainstay of the Bangladesh economy, contributing to the GDP, employment, and exports. During the Liberation War, in 1971, the damage to agriculture was estimated to be BDT 2400 million, and the government spent US$320.80 million to import 2.8 million Mt of rice and wheat (Samad 1983).

From 1972 to 1973, Bangladesh did not face serious floods or other natural calamities, and agricultural production increased by 11 percent. From July to August 1974, Bangladesh faced an unprecedented flood that severely damaged paddy crops and decreased employment opportunities, thereby affecting the purchasing power of the people who derived their livelihood from agriculture. Climatically, 1975 was a relatively good year, and food grain production increased by 14 percent (Samad 1983). Thus, managing natural disasters and improving agricultural production have, clearly, been the main concerns of planning in Bangladesh.

Bangladesh has followed a medium-term planning framework since 1973. Starting with the first FYP in July 1973, the country has, between 1973 and 2015, implemented a two-year plan and six FYPs and embarked on a seventh FYP (2015 to 2020). All the plans have attempted to put together various strategies and policies, bringing improvements in agriculture to generate rural employment, food security, and hence a reduction of national poverty. The planning effort, however, has been frustrated by frequent natural disasters such as floods, cyclones, and droughts, whose effect on food production during the different FYP periods is shown in Table 5.5.

The sixth FYP, from 2011 to 2015, was relatively disaster free, and the agricultural sector recorded an average growth of 4.5 percent, reflecting the country's success in attaining food security (GoB 2015).

Similarly to crops, noncrop constituents of agricultural production (i.e., forestry, livestock, and fisheries) also contribute significantly to the GDP and labor force employment, both of which are equally vulnerable to natural calamities like floods, cyclones, droughts, and salinity. Table 5.6 shows the contribution of the agricultural sector to the GDP in different fiscal years.

The growth of the agricultural sector in Bangladesh is declining on account of industrialization and urbanization, but its contribution to the economy is about 19 percent (GoB 2011), and it continues to play a very important role in the country's economy. Inasmuch as the growth performance of agriculture depends mainly on the weather, and is influenced by natural disasters, this sector remains fraught with uncertainties and vulnerabilities. Hence, sustaining agricultural production and building resilience to natural calamities have been the ongoing key issues

Table 5.5 State of food grain production

Five-year plan	Target production (Mt)	Actual production (Mt)	Shortfall (Mt)	Main cause of shortfall
First FYP 1973–1978	15.14	13.11	2.03	Owing to natural calamities like floods in 1974 and 1975, cyclone in 1974 and 1975, and drought in 1975.
Second FYP 1980–1985	17.50	15.80	1.70	Owing to floods in 1984, cyclone in 1981, 1983, and 1984, and drought in 1979, 1981, 1982, and 1984.
Third FYP 1985–1990	20.60	18.75	1.85	Owing to floods in 1978, 1987; consecutive severe floods in 1988; cyclone in 1985, 1986, and 1988; and drought in 1989.
Fourth FYP 1990–1995	21.98	19.07	2.91	Owing to natural calamities like floods in 1993, devastating cyclone in 1991, severe drought in 1994, and salinity.

Source: GoB (1998).

Table 5.6 Contribution of agriculture to GDP (%)

Sub-Sectors	2005–2006	2006–2007	2007–2008	2008–2009	2009–2010	2014–2015
Crops	11.09	11.49	15.25	15.06	14.98	16.00
Livestock	2.36	2.36	2.30	2.36	2.42	1.70
Forestry	1.51	1.51	1.43	1.38	1.34	1.70
Fisheries	3.89	3.89	3.76	3.67	3.61	3.70
Total	14.97	15.35	15.25	15.06	14.98	23.10

Source: GoB (2009a, b, 2011, 2015).

of planning. Proper policy adaptation, crop diversification, and efficient water management are considered by the policy makers to be crucial elements in the drive to achieve sustainable agricultural growth. Thus, all the FYPs have envisaged a targeted increase in and expansion of agricultural production through flood control and drainage, expansion of irrigation, scientific use of fertilizer and generation of new high-yielding varieties of seeds, provision of institutional support, and structural change within the agricultural sector.

Water Management

Improvements in agriculture are essential for development as it ensures economic stability, since most people in Bangladesh earn their livelihood from agriculture; and this stimulates the demand for manufactured goods. Food grain production is the main activity within the agriculture sector, accounting for more than two-thirds of all production and engaging over 80 percent of the total cultivated land. Water resource management has been chosen to drive substantial growth In agricultural production, guided by the National Water Policy 1999, Coastal Zone Policy 2005, Bangladesh Water Act 2014, and Participatory Water Management Regulations 2014. Water resource management covers protection against floods in the monsoon season, river erosion, saline water intrusion, and water-related hazards (i.e., cyclones accompanied by storm surges in the coastal belt and irrigation in the dry and wet seasons).

With regard to water resource management, the Bangladesh Water Development Board (BWDB) has been proceeding with projects to bring flood-prone land under improved flood control and drainage facilities. Up to June 2014, BWDB completed 776 projects, making 6.2 million hectares of agricultural land flood free, reduced drainage congestion, provided irrigation facilities on 1,572 million hectares by creating the necessary infrastructure and hence producing a biannual increase of 10 million Mt of food grain. It has also reclaimed about 10,020 sq. km, or about 0.10 million hectare of land, from the Bay of Bengal, and constructed a 11,283-km-long embankment, of which 4,571 km was in the coastal area (GoB 2015). Owing to the implementation of these projects, Bangladesh has enjoyed many benefits: the creation of a secure environment for crop production; generation of rural employment; protection of land, including agricultural land, from river erosion; security from floods, drought, water logging, cyclones, storm surges, and saline intrusion; primary protection against the impact of sea level rise due to climate change; and augmentation of agro-based economic activities in a flood-free secure environment (GoB 2015). Against the target of 3.64 million hectares set during the fourth FYP period, 3.84 million hectares of flood land was brought under flood control, and the drainage facilities increased by 5.90 hectares in June 2009 (GoB 2011). Besides, BWDB, a Local Government Engineering Department (LGED), is another actor in the management of water resources, but on a small scale. From 1995 to 2015, LGED developed around 720 sub-projects for water resources with the participation of local stakeholders and communities. This improved the sustainable use of water resources in around 450,000 hectares of land in the subproject areas (GoB 2015). These small-scale management practices have been proven to improve food production and empowerment of women and have hence reduced poverty in that area.

Irrigation

The expansion of the irrigation systems has been the most important determinant of the country's agricultural growth in facing the challenge of damages to irrigation infrastructure by natural disasters. Irrigation has been supporting high-yielding crops, allowing Bangladeshi farmers to practice multiple cropping, freeing them from their dependence on the rain. Bangladesh faces continued stress on surface water during the dry season, and the situation is aggravated when a drought occurs. In the dry season, large quantities of subsoil water are extracted, and the available river water is used for irrigation. Groundwater irrigation has been the major driver of crop production which is based mostly on shallow tube wells (STW), although deep tube wells (DTW) are also being used as a supplementary source of irrigation. STWs cover over 5.5 million hectares of a total cultivated area of 8.0 million hectares of land (GoB 2015). Irrigation in the dry season has increased the country's rice production by more than 80 percent in the last two decades (GoB 2011). Extraction of large amounts of groundwater will result in the depletion of soil nutrients, and policy makers and experts are grappling with this issue, which, together with climate change, is recognized as a threat to the maintenance of the ecological balance. Government of Bangladesh has therefore come down heavily on the use of DTWs and is promoting the use of rainwater harvesting for irrigation, and, concurrently, the Directorate of Agricultural Extension (DAE) has been running an awareness building program among the farmers.

Fertilizer and High-Yielding Variety (HYV) Seeds

During the last few decades, a dramatic advance has been made in the global crop production with the balanced use of fertilizers and the development of new varieties of seeds with high yields. Fertilizer, considered one of the critical inputs for increased agricultural production, has experienced increased demand from farmers. In response to this demand, GoB ensures the production and timely supply of fertilizer at a subsidized rate to farmers (GoB 2015). The government also issues alerts on unscientific and imbalanced use of chemical fertilizers, which can cause land degradation and eventual decline in soil fertility and yield. The government has also been working toward the production of nature-friendly bio-fertilizers and has taken practical steps to encourage farmers to use a balanced fertilizer approach to achieve increased production and maintain soil fertility.

Bangladesh Agricultural Development Corporation (BADC) is the main agent in promoting the agricultural development of the country. BADC has concentrated its efforts on the production of HYV seeds of crops and non-crops, including forestry, livestock, and fisheries, in the seed farms; besides, it is also encouraging farmers to adopt contractual seed multiplication. The government has supported the effort by creating suitable infrastructure for the production of hybrid climate-resilient varieties of seeds and saline drought-tolerant varieties. It also provides training and technical assistance to farmers to extend improved methods of seed production. Bangladesh developed a high-yield saline-tolerant jute seed and cultivated land with the newly developed seeds under a pilot project in the Satkhira district, which has the largest area affected by saline intrusion in the country. The project brought forth a highly satisfactory yield response, which promises to change the scenario of jute production. Meanwhile, through the implementation of the HYV program, per acre crops production in Bangladesh has doubled since the 1970s (GoB 2015). About 50 percent of the crop area of the country is now under HYV. At current development rates, almost all the suitable land will soon come under the HYV network (GoB 2011). Table 5.7 shows the growth and improvement scenario of crop production resulting from the implementation of HYV.

Table 5.7 Improvement of crop production

Crops	Unit	Production 1974	Production 1978	Production 2011	Production 2015	Projected production 2021
Food grains	Million Mt	11.83	13.10	34.51	35.25	38.21
Potato	—	0.72	0.85	8.33	8.76	10.43
Oil-seeds	—	0.214	0.264	0.40	0.45	0.52
Pulses	—	0.208	0.236	0.23	0.26	0.31

Sources: Samad (1983), GoB (2015).

Agricultural Research

Agricultural growth depends largely on research and development. Bangladesh has established some autonomous research institutes such as the Bangladesh Rice Research Institute, the Bangladesh Agriculture Research Institute, the Bangladesh Jute Research Institute, the Seed Research and Development Institute (SRDI), and so on to conduct service-oriented research aimed at boosting agricultural growth. Agriculture research is a major area of the GoB's focus under its National Agricultural Research System (NARS), coordinated by the Bangladesh Agriculture Research Council (BARC). Continued growth in production in Bangladesh is envisaged from the ongoing emphasis on stress-tolerant climate change effects, diversification of natural disasters-resilient agricultural production, development of varieties/species, pest and disease management, and improved on-farm water management. Also, the Department of Agricultural Extension has been entrusted with acquiring state-of-the-art knowledge of technological diversification and transferring it to the farmers and obtaining feedback.

Moreover, the GoB has been providing institutional support to farmers for sustainable agricultural growth even when faced with common natural disasters. Financial credit is one of the most important components. Inadequate access to credit for poor and marginal farmers is a serious constraint on agricultural production, and the government has hence been trying to extend credit facilities at a lower interest through banking channels, cooperatives, and even nongovernment organizations (NGOs).

Legal Initiatives

Climate change is one of the well-known reasons for natural disasters in Bangladesh. In responding to environmental challenges, the GoB has developed and enacted the Bangladesh Climate Change Strategy and Action Plan (BCCSAP) 2009. The plan document sets out the probable impacts of climate change in Bangladesh and different adaptation strategies and outlines mitigation issues. To meet the challenge of climate change, this plan describes programs to build the capacity and resilience of the country within thematic areas such as food security, social protection, and health; comprehensive disaster management; infrastructure; research and knowledge management; mitigation and low carbon development; capacity building and institutional strengthening. A second response is the National Adaptation Program of Action (NAPA), which provides intervention measures such as adaptation to coastal crop agriculture to combat salinity; enhanced agricultural systems in flash flooding areas; coastal fisheries through the culture of salt-tolerant fish; fisheries in enhanced flood-prone areas. The third response is the National Plan for Disaster Management (NPDM), to be used to develop disaster linkages within the national and international drivers; articulate the long-term focus of disaster management; address the issues of risk reduction, capacity building, information management, climate change adaptation livelihood security, and so on. A fourth response is the Standing Orders on Disasters (SOD) 2010, which describes the role and responsibilities of agencies concerned with disaster risk reduction and emergency management and establishes necessary actions required for the implementation of a disaster management plan and model. These legal initiatives seem to be appropriate and meaningful in facing natural disasters and climate-resilient development with strategies, for sustainable agricultural growth, conservation and enhancement of biodiversity, use of surface water, reduction of floods risk and pursuing for effective flood and drought management and basin-wide trans-boundary river management.

Conclusion and Recommendations

Bangladesh is predominantly an agricultural country; the main objective of its planning thus envisages protecting agricultural production mostly from natural disasters. The country's environmental degradation due to global climate change is seen in the rising sea levels along the coastal belt. This may lead to inundation and the spread of salinity. Further, excessive and/or low rainfall will continue to cause floods and/or drought. To deal with the impact of climate change, GoB has taken all possible steps to reduce disaster risk and protect mainstream agricultural production from natural calamities and climate change issues in midterm planning and the budgetary process.

Geographically, Bangladesh is low-lying and flat and situated at the bottom of the mighty river network of the Ganges, the Brahmaputra, and the Meghna with a long coastal belt. Over 92 percent of annual rainfall in the region (including upper riparian) enters the Bay of Bengal through Bangladesh. The country has little control over this water, which is one of the critical factors in flood, drought, and salinity issues. Thus, Bangladesh has to pursue more bilateral and regional cooperation with upper riparian countries for effective water and basin trans-boundary management to reduce the impact of floods, drought, and salinity on agricultural growth.

Under the prevailing conditions, agricultural loss arising from natural disasters cannot be stopped or tempered by any ad hoc measures. With a view to mitigating disasters and minimizing losses, GoB should resort to the following measures:

A) forecasting, by issuing weather bulletins and warning signals and setting up an efficient system for the dissemination of disaster warning through institutional networks like BMD, SPARRSO, BWDB, radio, television, and Cyclone Preparedness Programme (CCP) to allow people and the government agencies concerned as well as NGOs to take proper steps to face the disaster and reduce losses;

B) organizing public education and community mobilization activities to promote greater awareness of the preparation for and response to disaster. A comprehensive *Disaster Management Program*, a multi development supported program jointly managed by the Ministry of Food and Disaster Management (MFDM), has been working since 2004 to improve awareness and education to reduce the risk of disasters;

C) building embankments in coastal areas and on riverbanks and ensuring their timely and proper maintenance to mitigate the rush of surge waters and reduce the harmful saline effects and flood damage;

D) making effective use of land with forestation with a community focus, particularly in the coastal belt, for the absorption and weakening of disasters such as cyclone/storm surges; and

E) adopting appropriate laws, standing orders, national-level policies, guidelines, and action plans with the aim of improving inter-sectoral coordination, arranging training, providing specialist disaster management services to the agencies concerned and weighting to climate change adaptation and disaster potentials considering the various issues related to disasters, including food security, social protection and health, comprehensive disaster management, infrastructure, research and knowledge management, mitigation and low carbon development, and capacity building and institutional strengthening.

Undoubtedly, natural disasters are a major threat to sustainable agricultural production, and their growing occurrence in Bangladesh cannot be eliminated but only reduced through appropriate measures. This is a priority issue before national policy makers in their planning exercise and creation of programs. The government has been utilizing the national resources to deal with the situation. The dominance of structural measures and billion-dollar investment is seen as the primary mode of promoting agricultural development. However, with the limited national resources available, not all mitigation tasks may be feasible. Bangladesh needs regional cooperation in undertaking water management initiatives and to promote evidence-based claims from the effect of global climate and its impact on disaster events resilience. However, intensifying global climate change is a threat to national development. Bangladesh would do well to work together with its neighbors in climate change management to protect and enhance their collective common interests in natural disaster risk reduction and climate change adaptive capacities.

References

Ahamed, S., M.M. Rahman, and M.A. Faisal. 2012. "Reducing Cyclone Impacts in the Coastal Areas of Bangladesh: A Case Study of Kalapara Upzila." *Journal of Bangladesh Institute of Planners* 5, pp. 185–97.

Ali, A., F.M. Islam, and R. Kuddus, eds. 1996. *Development Issues of Bangladesh.* Bangladesh: University Press Ltd. Dhaka.

Azad, A.K., K.M. Hossain, and M. Nasreen. 2013. "Flood-Induced Vulnerabilities and Problems Encountered by Women in Northern Bangladesh." *International Journal of Disaster Risk Science* 4, no. 4, pp. 190–99.

Banu, N. 2015. "Cyclone AILA: Immediate Challenge and Impact on Socio-Economy (Seminar Paper)." Presented in the 2nd World Conference on Disaster Management organized by Network of Asia Pacific Schools and Institute of Public Administration and Governance (NAPSIPAG) on 19–22 November in India.

Brammer, H. 1998. "Drought in Bangladesh: Lessons for Planners and Administrators." *Disasters* 11, no. 1, pp. 21–9.

Choudhury, M.N.S. 1998. *Disaster and Its Management: An Overview of Bangladesh* (Seminar Paper). Savar, Dhaka, Bangladesh: Bangladesh Public Administration Training Centre.

Dhaka Tribune. April, 2017. "Paddy Production Hit by the Flood in the Hoars." *Dhaka Tribune.*

George, S. 2017. "A Third of Bangladesh Under Water as Flood Devastation Widens." *CNN (Cable News Network).* https://edition.cnn.com/2017/09/01/asia/bangladesh-south-asia-floods/index.html (accessed September 1, 2017).

Government of Bangladesh. 1998. *Fifth Five Year Plan, 1997–2002.* Dhaka, Bangladesh: Planning Commission.

Government of Bangladesh. 2009a. *Enhancing National and Community Resilience- Integrating Disaster Risks Reduction and Climate Change Adaptation Measures into Development Planning and Processes in*

Bangladesh-Guide to Practice. Dhaka, Bangladesh: Ministry of Food and Disaster Management.

Government of Bangladesh. 2009b. *Practicing Gender and Social Inclusion in Disaster Risk Reduction, Directorate of Relief and Rehabilitation*. Dhaka, Bangladesh: Ministry of Food and Disaster Management.

Government of Bangladesh. 2010a. *Standing Orders on Disaster, Disaster Management Bureau, Disaster Management and Relief Division*. Dhaka, Bangladesh: Ministry of Food and Disaster Management.

Government of Bangladesh. 2010b. *National Plan for Disaster Management 2010-2015*. Dhaka, Bangladesh: Disaster Management Bureau, Disaster Management and Relief Division, Ministry of Food and Disaster Management.

Government of Bangladesh. 2011. *Sixth Five Year Plan (part-1) 2011-2015*. Dhaka, Bangladesh: Planning Commission.

Government of Bangladesh. 2013a. *Cyclone Shelter Construction, Maintenance and Management Policy 2011, Cyclone Shelter Construction, Maintenance and Management Policy 2011*. Dhaka, Bangladesh: Government of Bangladesh.

Government of Bangladesh. 2013b. *National Sustainable Development Strategy 2010-2021*. Dhaka, Bangladesh: General Economic Division, Planning Commission.

Government of Bangladesh. 2015. *Seventh Five Year Plan 2016-2020*. Dhaka, Bangladesh: Planning Commission.

Haque, C.F., and M.Q. Zaman. 1989. "Coping with River-bank Erosion Hazard and Displacement in Bangladesh: Survival Strategies and Adjustments." *Disasters* 13, no. 4, pp. 300–14.

Islam, A.F.M.S. 2005. *Disaster Management: Impact on Socio-Economy of Bangladesh* (Seminar Paper). Savar, Dhaka, Bangladesh: Bangladesh Public Administration Training Centre.

Islam, S.M. 1999. *A Critical Analysis of Legal and Administrative Systems of Disaster Management in Bangladesh* (Seminar Paper). Savar, Dhaka, Bangladesh: Bangladesh Public Administration Training Centre.

Japan International Cooperation Agency. 1999. *Country Report-Training Course on Seminar on Administration for Disaster Management (25-01-2000 to 25-02-2000)*. Savar, Dhaka, Bangladesh: Bangladesh Public Administration Training Centre.

Kumar, U., M.A. Baten, A.A. Masud, K.S. Osman, and M.M. Rahman. 2012. *Cyclone Aila: One Year On.* Dhaka, Bangladesh: Unnayn Onnesan-The Innovators.

Rawlani, A.K., and B.K. Sovacool. 2011. "Building Responsiveness to Climate Change through Community Based Adaptation in Bangladesh." *Mitigation and Adaptation Strategies for Global Change* 16, no. 8, pp. 845–63.

Samad, A. 1983. *Bangladesh: Facing the Future.* Dhaka, Bangladesh: A Samad, BRAC Printers.

The Daily Star. April, 2017a. "Declare Hoars as Affected Areas." *The Daily Star.*

The Daily Star. April, 2017b. "Havoc in Hoar." *The Daily Star.*

The Independent. December, 2017. "Impact of Recent Flood." *The Independent.*

CHAPTER 6

A Call for Action to Mitigate the Cost of Natural Disaster in the Agricultural Sector: A Case Study in India

Sanjeev Kumar Mahajan

Himachal Pradesh University, Shimla, India

Anupama Puri Mahajan

Independent Researcher and Writer, Shimla, India

Introduction

Of all countries, India has been observed to be the most vulnerable and prone to natural disasters because of three main reasons, namely, its topography, geoclimatic conditions, and the abject poverty of much of its population. The geographical statistics of India show that almost 54 percent of the land is vulnerable to earthquakes (Indian Red Cross Society n.d.). A recent report indicated that 360 million people will be exposed to direct and indirect hazards if greenhouse emissions remain unchecked (The Future We Don't Want—Greatest Cities 2018). The data shows that 60 percent of the net area under agriculture is exposed to drought, four crore hectares of land mass are vulnerable to floods, sub-Himalayan/Western Ghats are vulnerable to landslides, and the coastal states are prone to cyclones. Therefore, India has a wide range of laws and mechanisms in place to deal with such disasters. Thus, to reduce the impact of disasters, disaster management becomes an integral part of public administration (Ray 2001).

It is necessary to validate such mechanisms and make them efficient and effective. India has been aggressive in formulating policies and strategies concerning deterrence, extenuation, and efficient disaster management before and after a calamity. Article 21 of the Indian Constitution states that "no person shall be deprived of his life or personal liberty except according to procedure established by law" (*Constitution of India;* Government of India, n.d.). This makes it imperative that the government takes on the responsibility to carry out all functions needed to be resilient in the face of disasters and work toward reducing the impact on infrastructure, livelihoods, and health and well-being.

According to Article 38 of the Constitution of India, the government should ensure the safety and security of its citizens. The implication of Article 38 is that the government will work to establish social welfare of the citizens by creating a social order comprising social, economic, and political justice. All the institutions, which function to achieve this goal, must themselves be well-informed and also inform the citizens of the impending dangers that can befall them. In the event of such dangers, the state must take care of its citizens. The Indian Constitution also empowers the states and the union government through the concurrent list to make their own legislations on the subject under consideration.

Despite the various mechanisms available to have disaster risk management plans in place, it is extremely difficult to prevent damage to the agricultural sector, the national economy, and the people living in the rural areas, who are most vulnerable (FAO 2015), when a natural disaster strikes. People in the rural areas have limited access to infrastructure, resources, and participative decision making to cope effectively with their miserable conditions after disasters. It is a well-established fact that climate and agriculture are closely associated. The level of agricultural production depends primarily on the climate in most of the countries. Because of the high levels of carbon dioxide released into the air, future projections of climate change indicate increasing temperatures and varied rainfall, both of which will greatly impact the agricultural sector (Raghavan et al. 2016).

However, this futuristic prediction is coming true right now. We are witnessing floods in the deserts, losses of livestock, and the desertification of grasslands. The normal weather patterns are changing. The FAO's (2016) work on disaster risk reduction at the global, regional, national, and local levels is guided by the Sendai Framework for Disaster Risk Reduction (SFDRR) 2015–2030. It is clear from this document that between 2003 and 2013, 22 percent of the total damage and losses caused by natural calamities in the developing countries occurred in the agricultural sector (FAO 2016).It has also been observed that India and other South Asian countries are the worst affected by natural disasters.

Objectives of the Study

In this chapter, an attempt has been made to study the status of disaster management and governmental programs in the context of mitigation of and preparedness for disasters in the state of Himachal Pradesh. The broad objectives of this study are to assess the following:

1. Hazard and vulnerability profile of Himachal Pradesh and
2. The extent of damage due to heavy rainfall in the state.

Research Methodology

The methodology followed in this study was to utilize secondary data published by different government agencies and nongovernmental organizations. Hence, the approach was deductive in nature. The diagrammatic representation of the hazard profile is given in Figure 6.1.

It is evident from Figure 6.1 that hazards in Himachal Pradesh have been classified into five major categories, namely, hydro-meteorological, geological, industrial, man-made, and biological. The fact that heavy rainfall or flash floods wreak havoc on the agricultural sector, thus adversely affecting the economy, is ignored by all major agencies in India. Thus, in this chapter, the thrust is to study the impact of heavy rainfall as one of the forms of natural disasters in the agricultural sector. An attempt has been made to highlight the persisting gap between the occurrence of the disaster and the relief measures; and to rethink the concept of disaster management in a situation as it occurs in a state. The central theme of this study can be twofold:

1. Understanding disaster risks in Himachal Pradesh and
2. Evaluating the impact of the damage caused by monsoons over the years in the agricultural sector.

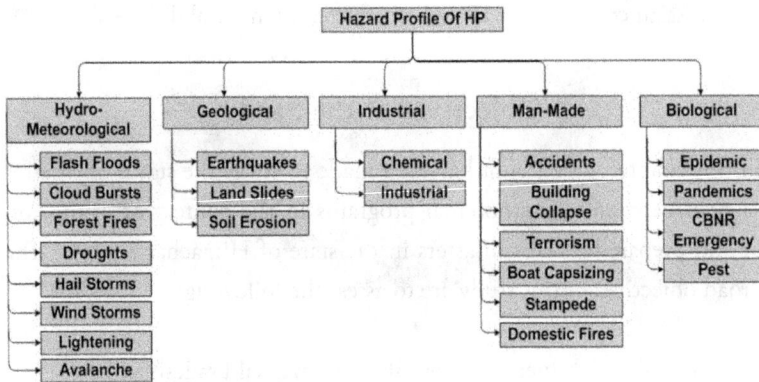

Figure 6.1 Hazard profile of Himachal Pradesh

Source: Himachal Pradesh State Policy or Disaster Management, 2011, p. 3.

Agriculture has been a powerful player in the development of the state and of the country as a whole. This study aims to fill the current gap relating to the examination of the impacts of disasters triggered by hazards in the agriculture sector. The major indicators are loss of human life, animal losses, houses damaged, damage to roads, damage to infrastructure facilities, and damage to agricultural and horticultural crops.

The state of Himachal Pradesh comprises 30 former princely states and the areas ceded by Punjab. Himachal Pradesh was constituted on April 15, 1948, 8 months after India's independence from British rule. It was declared a state of the Indian Union with Shimla, formerly

Table 6.1 Demographic features from 1901 to 2011

Year	Population	Decennial growth rate	Female per 1,000 males	Density per sq. km (persons)	Scheduled caste (percentage)	Scheduled tribes (percentage)
1901	1,920,294	—	884	34	—	—
1911	1,896,944	−1.22	889	34	—	—
1921	1,928,206	1.65	890	35	—	—
1931	2,029,113	5.23	897	36	—	—
1941	2,263,245	11.54	890	41	—	—
1951	2,385,981	5.42	912	43	22.69	0.26
1961	2,812,463	17.87	938	51	22.88	4.35
1971	2,460,434	23.04	958	61	22.24	4.09
1981	4,280,818	23.71	973	77	24.62	4.61
1991	5,170,877	20.79	976	93	25.34	4.22
2001	6,077,900	27.54	968	109	24.72	4.02
2011(P)	6,856,509	12.81	974	123	—	—

Source: Government of Himachal Pradesh (2014), p. 2.

Shimla, the summer residence of the British viceroy, as its capital on January 25, 1971.

The population is around 6.8 million (2011) (see Table 6.1). Its density is 123 people per square kilometer. The district-wise area density and decennial growth of the population in different districts is depicted in Table 6.2. It can be concluded from the given data that Himachal Pradesh is one of the smallest states. It is not as industrialized and developed as many other states of the Indian Union.

Regarding its scope, the study is confined to the disasters that took place in the period from 2013 to 2015, which hampered socioeconomic growth and development, which, in turn, pushed the state into a backward trajectory. Despite disaster management and relief legislations and mechanisms in place, the people were left in abject misery and hardship to survive the postdisaster phase. The efficient management of responses to disasters received increased attention both in India and from abroad (Government of Himachal Pradesh 2011). In this chapter, an attempt has been made to assess the damage caused due to rain during the monsoon period over the last few years.

Table 6.2 Area, density, and decennial growth population in different districts of Himachal Pradesh

Sr. No.	Districts	Area in sq. km	Total population		Decennial growth	Density per sq. km (2011)
			2001	2011 (P)		
1.	Bilaspur	1,167	340,885	382,056	12.08	327
2.	Chamba	6,528	460,887	518,844	12.58	80
3.	Hamirpur	1,118	412,700	454,293	10.08	406
4.	Kangra	5,739	1,339,030	1,507,223	12.56	263
5.	Kinnaur	6,401	78,334	84,298	7.61	13
6.	Kullu	5,503	381,571	437,474	14.65	79
7.	L&S	13,835	33,224	31,528	-5.10	2
8.	Mandi	3,950	901,344	999,518	10.89	253
9.	Shimla	5,131	772,502	813,384	12.58	159
10.	Simour	2,825	45,893	530,164	15.61	188
11.	Solan	1,936	500,557	576,670	15.21	298
12.	Una	1,540	448,273	521,057	16.24	338
13.	Himachal Pradesh	55,673	6,077,900	6,856,509	12.81	123

Source: Government of Himachal Pradesh 2016–2017, Statistical Abstract of Himachal Pradesh, Department of Economic & Statistics, Shimla, p. 27.

Findings and Discussions

The Indian economy largely depends on the agro sector (approximately, 70% of the population of India), which is not technically advanced and up-to-date when compared with international standards, and survives basically on monsoon rains. According to rough estimates, about 50 to 70 percent of the Indian population's livelihood comes from farming or agriculture-related activities. The contribution of the agricultural sector in India works out to be 18 percent of Gross Domestic Product (GDP) (Sector-wise Contribution GDP in India 2017).

Hazard and Vulnerability Profile of Himachal Pradesh

As mentioned earlier, Himachal Pradesh falls into the category of a high-risk zone for disasters—man-made as well as natural—comprising earthquakes, landslides, flash floods, snow storms and avalanche, droughts, and so on.

The impact of rainfall as a national disaster on the agricultural sector has not received proper attention in the period from 2013 to 2016, although abnormal levels of monsoon rains have impacted the lives of the farmers.

Profile of Agriculture in Himachal Pradesh

Himachal Pradesh is predominately a mixed farming state consisting of agropastoral, silvipastoral, and agrohorticultural on account of its hilly terrain. The state has 16,997 inhabited villages with 90 percent of the people living in the rural areas (Government of India 2016).

The state's agrarian economy is only a little over 10 percent of the total area which is cultivated. Population pressure on the cultivated land is high and the holdings of most of the cultivators are small and scattered—88 percent of the farmers are small and marginal, and their holdings are self-cultivated. About 20 percent of the cultivated area is under irrigation and the remaining 80 percent is rain fed (Government of Himachal Pradesh 2017).

The central focus of the study is on the issue surrounding small holdings and not on the irrigation facilities that are connected only to one-fifth of the total land. Hence, the farmers depend upon rainfall for their productivity. The characteristics of agroecological zones are depicted in Table 6.3.

Table 6.3 Characteristics of an agroecological zone

Character	Zone-I	Zone-II	Zone-III	Zone-IV
Ecology	Low hill sub-tropical	Mid hill sub-humid	High hill temperate wet	High hill temperate dry
Geographical area (0%)	35	32	25	8
Cropped area (0%)	33	53	11	3
Irrigated area (0%)	17	18	8	5
Altitude (MASL)	Up to 914	915–1,523	1,524–2,472	2,476–7,000
Rainfall (cm)	100–150	150–300	100–200	20–500
Area (Districts)	Kangra, Hamirpur, Solan, Sirmour	Kangra, Mandi, Solan, Shimla, Sirmour, Chamba	Kangra, Mandi, Sirmour, Shimla, Kullu, Bilaspur & Chamba	Lahaul & Spiti, Kinnaur, Chamba, Kullu

Source: Government of India (2005, p. 208).

This state has been classified into four agroecological zones on the basis of precipitation, altitude, and irrigation in the geographical area. Table 6.3 shows that 70 percent of the rainfall is observed during the monsoon season, but for the remaining part of the year there is water shortage in areas due to inadequate irrigation. Major crop areas lie in Zone II, where rainfall and irrigation are maximum, and the least are in Zone IV (Planning Commission 2005).

Table 6.4 depicts the distribution of operational land holdings and area operated by the size of class of holdings in Himachal Pradesh.

Table 6.4 Number of operational holdings and area operated by the size of class of holdings in Himachal Pradesh

Category	No. of holdings	Percent	Area (Hectare)	Percent
Marginal (less than 1 hectare)	670,425	69.78	273,270	28.63
Small (1.00–2.00 hectares)	174,596	18.17	243,942	25.55
Semi Medium (2.00–4.00 hectares)	84,868	8.83	230,469	24.14
Medium (4.00–10.00 hectares)	27,606	2.88	156,459	16.39
Large (10.00 hectares above)	3,270	0.34	50,511	5.29
Total all sizes	960,765	100.00	954,651	100.00

Source: Government of Himachal Pradesh 2015, Statistical Outline of Himachal Pradesh, Economics & Statistics Department, Shimla, Himachal Pradesh.

It is evident from Table 6.4 that 69.78 percent of operational holdings fall under the marginal category, that is, less than one hectare of about 97 percent of operational holdings, all less than four hectares, covering about 78 percent of the total area, which is classified into marginal, small, and semimedium categories on the basis of operations. Because of subdivision and fragmentation, land holdings have become unproductive. Hence, the holdings are scattered and are often unmanageable, and this becomes a limiting factor for crop production. Another major reason for this unproductivity is that 20 percent of land comes under irrigation by canals and tube wells, with the remaining 80 percent being dependent upon rainfall.

An Assessment of the Extent of Damage due to Monsoon

The state received heavy to very heavy rainfall during the period of this study. The extent of damage assessed, furnished in Table 6.5, is based on selected indicators. The details are as follows:

Loss of Human Lives

It is evident from Table 6.5 that the number of human lives lost during the period has shown an upward trend. It was 29 in the year 2013, followed by 45 in 2014 and 133 in 2015. Similarity, the total relief as compiled from records has seen a decline. It was Rs. 5.32 crores in 2015, and by August 2016, this figure had come down to Rs. 3.76 crores.

Loss of Animals

Table 6.5 shows that 23,449 animals including cows, sheep, and goats perished in 2013. The loss on this account was assessed at Rs. 4.05 crores. The loss in the years 2014 and 2015 was comparatively less, but by August 2016, an amount of Rs. 8.05 crores had been incurred as loss.

Houses Damaged

From Table 6.5, we can see that 3,246 houses were fully or partially damaged in different parts of Himachal Pradesh because of landslides triggered by heavy rain, and the overall loss of properties was assessed at Rs. 100.00 crores in 2013. The loss of the properties was less during the following years.

Damage to Roads

Many districts of the state received highly severe rainfall, which led to excessive damage to roads, bridges and culverts, and so on. Further, the monsoon caused huge landslides. Stretches of roads were washed away because of heavy and sudden inflow of rain water carrying slush and big boulders, blockage of cross-drainage, and blocking of roadside drains,

Table 6.5 Extent of damage

Sr. No.	Type of damage	2013 (Rs. in crore)		2014 (Rs. in crore)		2015 (Rs. in crore)		2016 (Rs. in crore)	
1.	Human lives lost	29	—	45	0.70	133	5.32	94	3.76
2.	Animals lost	23,449	4.05	698	0.22	686	0.59	81	8.05
3.	Houses damaged	3,246	100.00	127	3.71	3,364	6.59	1,004	4.61
4.	Damage to roads	4,100	1,046.00	336	450.00	—	404.27	—	187.46
5.	Damage to Irrigation & WS	2,263	214.12	2,726	120.00	5,307	214.52		78.46
6.	Damage to agriculture crops in Hectares	20,573	200.37	12,136	26.68		16.18		—
7.	Damage to horticultural crops (in hectare)	2.14	301.11	1550	173.40		104.00		
8.	Damage to electricity infrastructure		472.35		3.87		32.15		7.15
9.	Damage to community/ Govt. assets		165.00		50.00		2.55		3.08
10.	Loss to fisheries		5.00		—		0.75		—
11.	Total		2,508.45		828.86		786.92		292.56

Source: Government of Himachal Pradesh 2014, Memorandum of Damages Due to Heavy Rainfall in the State of Himachal Pradesh During Monsoon Season, Shimla, Revenue Department.

while landslides caused damage throughout the state. From Table 6.5, it can be seen that more than 4,100 roads in the state were affected during 2013, which led to a loss of Rs 1,046 crores in 2016. The damage to roads was assessed at Rs. 187.46 crores during the period covered.

Damage of Agriculture Crops

A majority of the population here depend on agriculture for their livelihood, with around 70 percent either directly or indirectly being involved in agricultural activities. About 20 percent of the income of the state comes from agricultural and allied sectors. As per the information given in Table 6.5, the extent of damage in the agriculture sector was high. The loss was assessed at Rs. 200.37 crores during 2013 and Rs. 214.52 crores in 2015. The assessment was carried out as per the National Disaster Response Force guidelines for assessing the loss of agricultural cropped area due to heavy rains.

Damage to Irrigation and Water Supply Schemes

The heavy rains during the period of study have resulted in a huge damage to the water supply, irrigation, sewerage, and flood control works. In Himachal Pradesh, the sources of water for most of the water supply and irrigation schemes are the khuds/nallahs(ravines)/rivers. During the monsoon, landslides cause damage to the assets of the schemes. Because of heavy rains, the loss was calculated to be Rs. 214.12 crores in 2013 and estimated at Rs. 78.46 crores in August 2016.

Damage to Horticultural Crops

Horticulture is an important sector contributing to the economic development in Himachal Pradesh, with about Rs. 3,000 crores being pumped into the economy (Government of Himachal Pradesh 2014). The horticultural sector in the state has a capacity to generate more income and employment. It is evident from Table 6.6 that many marginal, small, and other farmers were affected due to heavy rains. In certain parts, more than

Table 6.6 *Assessment of horticultural cropped area affected due to rains*

Year	Name of horticulture crop affected	Categorywise number of farmers affected				Categorywise affected areas (in hectares)				Total area affected where crop loss is more than 50%	
		No. of marginal farmers	No. of small farmers	No. of other farmers	Total no. of farmers	Marginal farmers	Small farmers	Other farmers	Total farmers	Quantitative loss (MT)	
2013	Fruits crops	48,472	18,572	12,623	79,667	26,422	12,220	3,435	42,077	24,145	2,244
2014	Fruits crops	18,912	10,499	11,731	41,002	8,204	3,712	4,418	17,474	3,171	9,827
2015	Fruits crops	27,562	9,746	4,271	41,579	16,963	7,900	4,881	29,744	10,465	5,460

Source: Government of Himachal Pradesh (2014, p. 23).

50 percent of crop loss was reported during the period of study because the horticultural industry is exposed to various types of weather vagaries like hailstorms, droughts, strong winds, and untimely and excessive rain. There was a huge loss of fruit crops in 2013. The losses calculated, as per the Government of India guidelines, amounted to Rs. 301.11 crores in 2013 and Rs. 173.40 crores in 2014.

Damage to Electricity Infrastructure

The electricity infrastructure was severely damaged in many of the districts of the state. The total loss was assessed at Rs. 472.35 crores in 2013 and Rs. 32.15 crores in 2015.

Damage to Community/Government Assets

A lot of community assets in the state like Bhawans, community centers, village paths, and so on were damaged during the monsoon. The total loss of these assets amounted to over Rs. 165 crores in 2013 and Rs. 50 crores in 2014.

Loss of Fisheries

Silt and flooding of rivers, lakes, and reservoirs caused a major damage to the fisheries sector. The total damage to the sector was assessed at the tune of Rs. 5 crores in 2013.

It can be concluded from this overview that rainfall during the monsoon season played havoc and caused destruction during the time period of the study. It not only resulted in loss of human lives but also contributed to huge economic losses. The monsoon plays a dominant role in Himachal Pradesh as it is an agrarian economy with 80 percent of the land holdings depending on rainfall, as has been said earlier. The state receives the majority of its rains during the monsoon season, although, because of the topographical conditions, certain areas receive normal to above normal rainfall resulting in the loss of human lives, animal lives, and others as mentioned in Tables 6.5 and 6.6.

Mechanisms for Calculation of Assistance

The manual on Administration of the State Disaster Fund and The National Disaster Response Fund (2013) has formulated criteria to measure and evaluate the assistance required. The government of Himachal Pradesh asked for financial assistance from central agencies. In 2014, an amount of Rs. 4,500 was sought for the rain-fed agricultural areas. It was Rs. 9,000 for the agricultural irrigated area and Rs. 12,000 for the perennial category of crops. The government calculated the total loss arising out of agricultural input subsidy for the small and marginal farmers on the basis of the approved rates. Accordingly, an assessment of horticultural cropped area along with loss of agricultural and horticultural land is assessed.

Present Institutional and Legal Arrangement

The national policy concerning disasters has been formulated under the guidance of the National Vision to establish a safe environment for people that has strong resilience to disaster. The Disaster Management Act 2005 was passed to provide for effective management of disasters and other related issues. It has established the institutional, legal, financial, and coordination mechanisms at the national, state, district, and local levels. The main objective is to efficiently and effectively manage disaster preparedness, prevention, and the minimizing of the impact of the disaster. The National Disaster Management Authority, (National Disaster Management Authority, 2015) with the Prime Minister as its head, as the apex body at the national level for disaster management was established "to build a safer and disaster resilient India by a holistic, pro-active, technology driven and sustainable development strategy that involves all stakeholders and fosters 'a culture of prevention, preparedness and mitigation" (National Policy on Disaster Management 2009).

State Disaster Management Authority

At the level of each state, the State Disaster Management Authority (SDMA), under the chairmanship of the chief minister, is responsible for disaster management. The chief secretary is the chief executive officer of the SDMA, who is responsible for coordination and implementation of response to disasters.

Various departments of the state ensure the integration of prevention, preparedness, and mitigation measures, capacity building, and preparedness of the departments (Government of Himachal Pradesh 2011).

The State Executive Committee

The role of the State Executive Committee (SEC) is to coordinate and monitor the implementation of the national plan and the state plan. The SEC also provides the necessary technical assistance to district authorities to carry out their functions properly and effectively.

State and District Crisis Management Group

The purpose of the State Crisis Management Group (SCMG) and District Crisis Management Group (DCMG) normally is to handle crisis situations arising out of disasters. Similarly, at the district level, the District Disaster Management Authority (DDMA) has been created to identify the areas vulnerable to disasters and measures for the prevention of disasters and the mitigation of the effects with the help of local authorities (Government of Himachal Pradesh 2011). The DDMA is headed by the district collector, and includes elected representatives and other officials to carry out its activities effectively.

Future Requirements

In this study, an effort has been made to understand the impact of monsoons on disasters. Therefore, an effective disaster management must focus on minimizing the loss of lives and property. It is beyond the control of mankind to stop disasters, but action must be taken to reduce the risks through innovative, timely, and effective measures. Some of the major requirements for minimizing the adverse effects of disasters are given in the following paragraphs.

Need to Understand the Nature

It is pertinent to understand the nature and characteristics of disasters. Disaster risk reduction and management strategies should be systematically embedded into the agricultural sector. Accordingly, the plans and the required investment should be pumped in, especially in a state like

Himachal Pradesh where agriculture is a critical source of livelihood of the people.

Agricultural Insurance and Compensation of Losses

Crop insurance should be made compulsory, so that it becomes a logical means to provide compensation and incentive to farmers to avoid the losses arising from disasters. The insurance agencies and the state governments should work together in reducing the losses and assessing the compensation to the affected people on time. The claims should be settled within a prescribed time limit to avoid any hardships to the people.

Warning Systems

Warning systems should be in place in all major cities/towns and villages. These monitoring systems can be utilized to protect the residents' lives and property. Awareness campaigns about the utility of the warning systems should be carried out extensively in the state. This will work as a confidence-building measure among the residents of the state.

Increased Financial Resources

Increased financial resources for the victims of disasters should be on the agenda of any nation or state. It should be particularly directed toward the agricultural sector, where the economy is based on the agriculture. The government should also rope in the private sector in dealing with this problem under the umbrella of corporate social responsibility. This will help in achieving sustainable agricultural growth and, in turn, will lead to better economic growth.

Reducing Risks from Flash Floods

It is evident from the discussion that monsoon triggers flash floods in the country every year. Almost as many as 10 Indian states are under the negative impact of floods at the present time. Hence, the states should develop comprehensive policies and plans to link rivers across the country. Accordingly, the capacity of the institutions should be enhanced effectively to implement the plans.

Role of Communities and Local Government

Local residents and local bodies like panchayats and municipalities should be consulted for the preparedness, planning, and relief and rehabilitation work. Local bodies are the most appropriate institutions, from the local level to the district, in view of its proximity. Their involvement will help in countering disasters as well as taking preventive and protective activities to mitigate the impact of disasters. It is the right time to define the role of local bodies and sensitize the communities regarding preparedness and mitigation measures of disasters to minimize the destruction of life and property.

It can be observed that disasters cannot be prevented, but their impact on the residents' lives and properties can be reduced to the maximum extent possible. Such a step will also help mitigate socioeconomic problems to a large extent. The main responsibility lies with the national and state governments to identify their roles to help people in crisis. Lastly, the people themselves should play a greater role with a sense of responsibility to face disasters bravely rather than depending solely on state governments. In this connection, governments need to focus more on how to handle situations arising out of disasters in their states. The disaster plan should investigate the problem areas and take corrective actions.

References

Department of Revenue, Government of Himachal Pradesh. 2011. *Himachal Pradesh State Policy on Disaster Management*. Shimla, HP: Disaster Management Authority.

Food and Agriculture Organization of the United Nations. 2015. *Planning Communication for Agricultural Disaster Management*. Rome, France: Food and Agriculture Organization of the United Nations.

Food and Agriculture Organization of the United Nations. 2016. *Disaster Risk Reduction in Agriculture*. Rome, France: Food and Agriculture Organization of the United Nations. www.fao.org/policy-support/policy-themes/disaster-risk-reduction-agriculture/en

Government of Himachal Pradesh. 2011. *Activity Report*. Shimla, HP: Revenue Department.

Government of Himachal Pradesh. 2014. *Memorandum of Damages Due to Heavy Rainfall in The State of Himachal Pradesh*. Shimla, HP: Revenue Department, p. 10.

Government of Himachal Pradesh. 2017. *Annual Action Plan 2017-18.* Shimla, HP: Department of Agriculture, p. 4.Government of India. 2005. *Himachal Pradesh Development Report.* New Delhi: Planning Commission, p. 208.

Government of India. 2016. *Himachal Pradesh Development Report.* Shimla: State Planning Division, Planning Commission, p. 207.

Government of India. n.d. *Constitution of India.* India: Government of India. http://www.india.gov.in/my-governemnt/constituion-india/constitution-india-full-text

Government of India. n.d. *Registrar General and Census Commissioner.* http://censusindia.gov.in/2011-Common/CensusData2011.html 2011 Census Data.

Indian Red Cross Society. n.d. *Earthquake in Nepal & Adjoining Indian States.* New Delhi: Indian Red Cross Society.

Ministry of Statistics and Programme Implementation, Planning Commission, Government of India. 2017. *Sector-wise Contribution of GDP in India.* Ministry of Statistics and Programme Implementation, Planning Commission, Government of India. statisticstimes. com/economy/sectorwise-gdp-contribution-of-india.php

National Disaster Management Authority. 2009. *National Policy on Disaster Management.* https://ndma.gov.in/images/guidelines/national-dm-policy 2009.pdf

National Disaster Management Authority. 2015. *NDMA Vision.* National Disaster Management Authority. https://ndma.gov.in/en/

Raghavan, S.V., J. Ze, J. Hur, L. Jiandong, N.S. Nguyen, S. Yabin, and L. Shie-Yuie. 2016. *Distributional Impacts of Climate Change and Food Security in South Asia.* ERIA Discussion Paper 2016-41. Jakarta, Indonesia. Retrieved from http://www.eria.org/catalogue-2017-agriculture-and-disaster-management.pdf

Ray, C.N. 2001. *Earthquake Relief and Rehabilitation in Gujarat: Issues in Disaster Management in The Indian Journal of Public Administration.* Vol. XLVIII. Delhi: Indian Institute of Public Administration. p. 129.

UCCRN. 2018. "The Future We Don't Want: How Climate Change Could Impact the World's Greatest Cities." https://www.downtoearth .org.in/news/360-million-people-will-be-exposed-to-extreme-heat-in-142-indian-cities-by-2050-60903

CHAPTER 7

Food Security through Public (Food) Distribution System in a Postdisaster Situation: A Comparative Study of Bangladesh and West Bengal (India)

Rabindranath Bhattacharyya

Department of Political Science, University of Burdwan

Jebunnessa

Department of Public Administration, Jahangirnagar University

Introduction

Natural disasters occur only when natural hazards happen in a vulnerable situation. For instance, if any natural hazard like earthquake hits an uninhabited desert area, there will be no loss of life or livelihood. But if such an earthquake hits a highly populated city, it will lead to loss of human lives as well as loss of lives of domestic animals and a huge loss of property and assets. Of course, the degree of such loss would be determined by the capacity of the people living in the area to anticipate such a disaster and to take necessary steps to reduce its impact. If the area is inhabited by a large number of vulnerable people like the aged, children, or disabled who cannot move easily or if the social network remains weak in providing help for emergency evacuation of the people, the impact of such natural hazards will be huge, to be termed as natural disasters. This way, natural disaster is natural hazard combined with vulnerability. Wisner et al. (2004) define vulnerability as "the characteristics of a person or group and their situation that influence their capacity to anticipate, cope with, resist and recover from the impact of a natural hazard (an extreme natural event or process)" (p. 11). Age, income, social network, or neighborhood characteristics all lead to vulnerability to disaster (Flanagan et al. 2011; Tapsell et al. 2010). Normally the policy makers emphasize upon the first part, that is, how to reduce the risk of hazard, because the policy planners have scanty knowledge in specifying those characteristics of a group that make them vulnerable to hazard. This leads to overgeneralization of a concrete disaster or postdisaster situation and to the lack of social capacity building for risk governance. But whatever be the causes of vulnerability, it ultimately leads to the lack of three basic securities/needs: food, shelter, and livelihood.

Thus, this chapter is an attempt to explore to what extent the existence of a stable and operational public distribution network may ensure food security in a postdisaster situation, on the basis of a comparative study between Bangladesh and West Bengal (India) that has been necessitated by homogeneous topographic, ecological, environmental, and cultural traits of Bangladesh and West Bengal. A large province of Bengal was divided by the British in 1905 "into a western part ('Bengal') and an eastern part ('Eastern Bengal and Assam')" (Schendel 2009, p. 79), which was later united in 1911. In 1947 after achieving independence from the British, Pakistan was separated from India and East Bengal became a province of Pakistan. In 1955 East Bengal was renamed as East Pakistan and in 1971 East Pakistan became independent from Pakistan (Schendel 2009, p. 96) and took the official name People's Republic of Bangladesh (commonly known as Bangladesh). West Bengal and Bangladesh thus share a common topography, common ecology, common environmental hazards like flood caused either by incessant rains or by tidal surge due to cyclones, and of course a common language and a common cultural and historical heritage. With these similarities in view, a comparative study of food security in postflood situation has been attempted in this chapter that may lead to the building of a replicable model on implementation of programs for food security in a postdisaster situation for developing countries.

The research questions that this chapter attempts to explore are:

1. How does the network of Public Distribution System (PDS) in West Bengal (India) and in Bangladesh in distributing food grains operate in a sustainable manner, especially in a postdisaster situation?
2. To what extent does the PDS in these two countries ensure food security in a postdisaster situation, especially after the first phase of the crisis is over?
3. What else are required for making the PDS more effective in a postdisaster situation?

The chapter is based on secondary data collected from government reports and publications, reports of international organizations, and relevant books and journals. There are two key areas in this chapter for which data were to be collected: (i) the occurrences of flood in West Bengal and Bangladesh and its impact on the people in the postdisaster situation especially in respect of food security, and (ii) the sustainability of the public distribution network in delivering food during the postdisaster situation in those countries. But the limitation of the government record for both the countries is that the data that have been kept in public domain are neither comprehensive regarding the occurrences of floods and their impact in terms of food security nor updated. This is true about the National Disaster Management Authority (NDMA) of India portal, West Bengal Disaster Management Authority (WBDMA) portal, the Ministry of Statistics and Programme Implementation, Government of India's portal, as well as the disaster management department's portal of the Government of Bangladesh. For example, the Disaster Data and Statistics page in the NDMA website presents a table along with a heading "Some major disasters in India" in which a few disasters in some of the 29 states and 7 union territories since the year 1972 up to 2014 have been presented in 30 rows and 4 columns incoherently. The West Bengal Disaster Management & Civil Defence Department (WBDM & CD) portal has presented the sequence of floods since 1978 up to 2013, although why flood occurrences in 2008, 2009, and 2011, when a large number of people were affected, have been left out of this table remains unknown. Bangladesh Bureau of Statistics (2016) has presented data regarding disasters from 2009 to 2014 in a booklet in an analytical way, although there is a dearth of yearwise data distribution. Hence, regarding the record of flood instances and its impact, the author had to compile data from relief reports and assessment reports of nongovernment organizations such as ReliefWeb, Oxfam, and Save the Children, other than government records, although in comparing the data of the two countries in terms of specific year and units of analyses such data provided by the authors remain limited. The Food Security portal facilitated by the International Food Policy Research Institute (IFPRI) as well as the Asian Development Bank and the World Bank research papers has been used in this chapter as one of the major sources of general information as well as background research reports of food security in both India and Bangladesh, while the official portal of the West Bengal Public Distribution System and the official Food Planning and Monitoring Unit portal of the Ministry of Food have served as the government records regarding the beneficiaries of the public distribution system. The Government of Bangladesh has provided the government records regarding the beneficiaries of the PDS. The unavailability of flood insurance data or compensation data in the government domain in Bangladesh has made the assessment of flood damage in Bangladesh limited in nature.

Key Issues

Flood causes damage of crops, crop lands, and thereby leads to temporary loss of livelihood and income of those who are dependent on agriculture. The situation becomes critical if in such situations people on the one hand lack formal disaster insurance mechanisms and on the other cannot cope with the impact of flood by informal risk-sharing mechanisms, including micro-insurance, because of the magnitude of the damage caused by the disaster. "(I)n the case of Bangladesh, formal insurance mechanisms for catastrophes are very poorly developed, and traditional informal mechanism of risk-sharing is unable to respond when major natural disasters occur" (Ozaki 2016, p. 1). Also, Bangladesh has "limited budgetary resources and limited markets to support the proactive transfer of catastrophe risk" (Ozaki 2016, p. 1). In India, however, there are various insurance coverage schemes viz. the Modified National Agricultural Insurance Schemes (MNAIS), Pradhan Mantri Fasal Bima Yojana (PMFBY), and the Restructured Weather-Based Crop Insurance Scheme (RWBCIS) for the damage or loss of crops due to flood or draught. Data reveal that during 2010–2011 to 2015–2016, the number of farmers covered for Rabi crop in West Bengal under MNAIS was 1,943,351 (323,892 on an average per year). And during 2016, the number of farmers covered for Kharif crop in West Bengal was 308,9434 under PMFBY and 1,700 under RWBCIS (Government of India 2017). Consequently, food security remains the key issue in a postflood situation. Various policy options such as agricultural insurance, micro-insurance, gratuitous cash relief, and PDS are available to address that issue. However, in the context of limited budgetary resources of a country, PDS may act as an effective tool in providing food security in a postdisaster situation.

Government concern for the management of disaster focusing on the capacity building, prompt responses to any threats of disaster, assessment of the impact of disasters, and rehabilitation and reconstruction in the postdisaster situation is a recent phenomenon both in India and in Bangladesh. In a concerted way, government initiatives for disaster management started in India since the passing of the Disaster Management Act 2005. In Bangladesh, such Disaster Management Act was passed in 2012. That may be one of the major reasons for the dearth of comprehensive books, specifically on food security in a postdisaster situation or, more generally, on disaster management in both India and in Bangladesh. Nevertheless, recent attempt to explore disaster risk reduction (Pal and Shaw 2018) is relevant in this context. Two chapters in that book have discussed the risk-reduction issues of West Bengal and Bangladesh. In chapter 6 (by Maitra), the focal point of the analysis is the role of disaster management department of the Government of West Bengal in view of the shift of focus from crisis management to disaster risk reduction. Statistics of cyclones and floods in West Bengal, as mentioned by the WBDMA, have been presented here along with the statistics of earthquakes and landslides of West Bengal. Thereafter, the mechanisms to mitigate the challenges posed by such disasters have been discussed. Chapter 12 (Pal and Ghosh 2018) has discussed the details of various structural and nonstructural measures adopted for disaster risk reduction in the wake of Aila cyclone in the Sundarbans region in West Bengal.

Disaster Law Emerging Thresholds (2018), edited by Amita Singh, has explored through 24 chapters the appropriate legal frameworks for reducing risks of disasters and institutional reforms toward capacity development for community resilience. Chapter 5 of this book by Ahmad has reviewed the disaster law and community resilience in Bangladesh, concentrating on the risk profile and disaster policy of the country. Chapter 22 (Bhattacharyya) has discussed the limitations in implementing laws in reality in reducing disaster risk, with a case study of Mandarmani sea beach in West Bengal.

The book titled *Strategic Disaster Risk Management in Asia*, edited by Huong Ha et al. (2015), contains 15 chapters revealing various issues of disaster risk management viz. the role of the polity, the administration, the armed forces, and the community in building capacity for risk reduction, preparedness for responding to disaster, and reconstructing the postdisaster scenario in the context of India, Bangladesh, Sri Lanka, and Philippines. In Chapter 2 (Banu), an assessment of the steps and programs in the five-year plans for the reduction of risks and responses to the consequences of disaster in Bangladesh has been attempted. Chapter 9 (Bhattacharyya) has focused on the political and administrative reconstruction process in post-Aila (cyclone) Sundarbans region, with a case study of Bally II Gram Panchayat in Gosaba block.

Chakraborty et al. (2013), on the basis of a micro study of the Debhog Gram Panchayat in Sabang administrative block of Paschim Medinipur district in West Bengal, have analyzed the nature and effects of floods on the people along with the government policies to natural disasters and have attempted to develop a conceptual framework on the basis of vulnerability.

Although the authors could not find any book/report (government or nongovernment) establishing the relationship between PDS and food security of the flood-ravaged victims or so to say of any disaster either in India or in Bangladesh, there are many reports, discussion papers, and individual research papers on PDS in India as well as in Bangladesh. The report by the NITI Aayog Development Monitoring and Evaluation

Office, Government of India (2016), has made a comparative study of 2004–2005 and 2011–2012 panel data in showing the coverage, access, and use of Targeted Public Distribution System (TPDS), the role of TPDS and Antyodaya Anna Yojana (AAY) in determining the nature of food consumption in view of an increase or a decrease in income, and the efficiency of the PDS. The report, although has not established any link between the impact of disasters and the decrease in income, has recommended for initiating cash transfer as a pilot program in a few districts through PDS because it has found that "cash subsidies instead of in-kind subsidies via the PDS could enhance dietary diversity" (NITI Aayog, Government of India 2016, p. viii). Even if quite dated, in a long World Bank discussion paper on PDS in India (1997), Radhakrishna and Subbarao (1997) discussed the prospect of a reformed and restructured TPDS, which was then newly initiated, in view of three aspects: (i) incidence of fallen poverty in the context of faster serial production than demand; (ii) growth of well-developed and integrated agricultural marketing infrastructure; and (iii) development of Panchayati Raj as decentralized democratic institutions that might take the responsibility of implementing poverty alleviation programs.

In an analytical report on PDS in India, Balani (2013) wrote that in India National Food Security Act (2013) rests on the existing TPDS mechanism to deliver these entitlements. In that report, Balani has shown several gaps in the implementation of TPDS. These include inaccurate identification of households in inclusion or exclusion of targeted beneficiaries and a leaking delivery system. Such lacunae get increased by the fact that the National Food Security Act 2013 does not mention the disaster-hit people within the targeted groups of public distribution. Thus, in case of a postdisaster situation, the gaps in implementation of said Act increase, and leading to relief distribution politics as well.

Habiba et al. (2015) edited the book titled *Food Security and Risk Reduction in Bangladesh* that contained 15 chapters. The book by drawing the experiences of various national- and community-level programs has discussed the challenges for ensuring food security and their implications for risk reduction in Bangladesh. Chapter 13 (Parvin) has addressed the vital issues of climate change, flood, food security, and human health, with an interconnected dimension in Bangladesh.

In a 227-page-long Bangladesh development series paper (No. 31), the World Bank (2013) has made an assessment of reducing poverty in Bangladesh during 2000–2010. In that series paper, chapters 7 and 8 has elaborately discussed the repercussions of food price shocks on wages, welfare, and policy responses and the role of safety nets to cope with the vulnerabilities. In chapter 8, there is a section on the public food distribution system in Bangladesh, which was established in the wake of the Bengal famine of 1943. The objectives of the public food distribution system (PFDS) as mentioned there are basically three maintenances, namely,(i) security stock in case of emergencies and weather-related shocks, (ii) stability of food prices, and (iii) food security for the poor population (World Bank 2013). The paper also revealed the data regarding an increase in food grain stock and distribution. "The 2010-11 target for public distribution increased to 2.29 million tons, and in 2011-12, it was 2.1 million tons. Currently, public stocks total 2.77 million" (World Bank 2013, p. 104). Although there was an increase in the stock of food, the paper indicated the deterioration of the quality of PFDS food grain and leakage of food distribution, the impact of which is borne by the safety net beneficiaries.

In the chapter on PFDS in Bangladesh, Ali et al. (2008) compared the food policy of India with that of Bangladesh and the benefits that Bangladesh got in procuring rice in the post-1998 flood situation. The three underlying objectives of PFDS in Bangladesh, as they viewed, are (i) implementation of ceiling prices,(ii) poverty alleviation and food security for all vulnerable groups, and (iii) disaster management.

One major Bangladesh–India initiative was taken by the International Union for Conservation of Nature (IUCN) titled Situation Analysis on Floods and Flood Management, where Prasad and Mukherjee (2014) underlined five broad thematic areas, and the first among these areas is "food security, water productivity and poverty" (p. 3). The IUCN concentrated on creating "situation analyses" on each thematic area and related issues. The analysis that the IUCN has taken is thorough and deep probing in identifying core issues and their significance within the India–Bangladesh geographic focus. But the analysis has not focused on the PDS system of both the countries for ensuring food security during postflood situation.

On the basis of the above review of literature, it may be said that there is a dearth of literature linking the operations of PDS in a postdisaster situation as a mechanism to respond to the impact of disaster whether in India or in Bangladesh. Nevertheless, the literature on PDS is based on the good governance discourse that focuses on the role of government in delivering service for and ensuring accountability to the citizens for sustainable food security. In a postdisaster situation, the government faces the vulnerabilities of the population in a much broader way, and hence the government should have the capacity to plan and prepare for response, to coordinate assistance, and to develop policies on food security.

Flood and Food Security

For the healthy well-being of a people, nutritious food is required. That is not possible without a certain level of income and accessibility of the food in the area. Disasters always have a direct impact on the various livelihoods that put the income of the disaster-hit people in jeopardy. This is more so in rural society in developing countries (FAO 2015). Food security and livelihood in India and Bangladesh, both being developing countries, get affected in case of disaster. Going by topography, Bangladesh and West Bengal, a constituent state in the eastern part of India, are akin to each other. Consequently, the nature of disasters that hit West Bengal is of similar nature to the disasters that hit Bangladesh. Cyclones often have a trailing route to both West Bengal and Bangladesh, originating from the Bay of Bengal, creating tidal surge, and thereby resulting in flood. Likewise, because of heavy rains, floods are also common in West Bengal and Bangladesh. Incidentally, both these areas depend heavily on agriculture for livelihood.

Agriculture and allied sectors are the largest employers in both West Bengal and Bangladesh. In West Bengal, about 39 percent of the total workforce and about 70 percent of the total population depend on agriculture for their livelihood. Also agriculture contributes to 20.34 percent of the net state domestic product (Bengal Chamber of Commerce 2013). On the other hand, "Agriculture provides livelihoods for over 60% of the population of Bangladesh. However, people living in the flash flood and drought prone districts in the northwest and the saline affected tidal surge areas in the south struggle year after year to produce enough to eat or earn a living" (World Bank 2013, p.38). Since in both the countries flood occurs almost regularly, a huge number of people, as found in Tables 7.1 to 7.4, become affected at different levels with regard to their livelihood and income. In postdisaster situations, the affected people face the basic problem of food security because of the temporary loss of work and the basic problem of the administration remains to distribute food grains in a sustainable manner especially after the first phase of crisis is over. Although there has been no study linking the postdisaster impact on the livelihood and income of the flood-affected people in West Bengal or in Bangladesh, on the one hand, and their food security status, on the other, it may be deduced that the impact on the flood-affected people's livelihood and income is bound to put impact on food security. IFPRI (2009) in their study on Indian State Hunger Index (ISHI) placed West Bengal in the 8th place among 17 states in India, with the ISHI score of 20.97 (comparable Global Hunger Index [GHI] Rank 60, although India got Rank 66 with a score of 23.7), which was "alarming." Bangladesh was compared with West Bengal in that report as having 25.2 score (with GHI Rank 70). After 2009, there was no other study on ISHI either by IFPRI or by any other organization. But the GHI 2017 shows Bangladesh with the rank of 88 (GHI score 26.5) and India with the rank of 100 (GHI score 31.4) (IFPRI 2017, p.13). This means the food security status of both the countries has deteriorated.

Table 7.1 Household, population, and household size in disaster-prone areas in Bangladesh

Division	Household	Population			Percentage (%)			Household size
		Total	Male	Female	Total	Male	Female	
1	2	3	4	5	6	7	8	9
Bangladesh	4,361,261	20,204,367	10,497,444	9,706,923	100.00	51.96	48.04	4.63

About 13% of households and 12.64% of the population live in disaster-prone areas of the country. Household size is slightly larger (4.63) than the national size (4.44).
Source: Bangladesh Bureau of Statistics [BBS] (2016), p. 5.

Table 7.2 The distribution of disaster-affected households by division and disasters, 2009–2014

Division	Total household	Drought	Flood	Water logging	Cyclone	Tornado	Storm/tidal surge	Thunderstorm	River/coastal erosion	Landslides	Salinity	Hailstorm	Others (e.g., Insecticides)
1	2	3	4	5	6	7	8	9	10	11	12	13	14
Bangladesh	4,361,261	14.80	34.48	13.88	21.31	4.14	8.65	14.94	4.95	0.08	4.09	11.88	7.90

Source: Bangladesh Bureau of Statistics (BBS) (2016), p. 8.
NB. Other than insecticides all other types are directly related to occurrences of flood.

Table 7.3 The percentage of flood-prone areas and flood-affected victims in West Bengal, 2009–2017

Division	Total population	Total no. of people affected by flood during these years	Percentage of flood victims	Total area	Flood-prone area	Percentage of flood-prone area	Percentage of net cropped area identified as flood prone
West Bengal	91,276,115 (2011 census)	18,586,539 approx.	20.36	88,752 sq. km.	37,660 sq. km flood-prone area spread over 111 blocks	42.43	69

Source: West Bengal Disaster Management Department (2018).

According to Bangladesh Disaster Census report during 2009–2014, the average nonworking days per household due to flood was 17.63, and the total percentage of nonworking days due to flood was 26.93 (BBS 2016, p. 9). During that period, the amount of total losses and damages has been calculated at 42,807.19 million taka, and that is 23.23 percent of the total losses and damages incurred by other natural disasters (BBS 2016, p. 10). The report has also mentioned that, during the Financial Years 2009–2015, the average annual GDP volume is 11,378,286 million BDT (BBS 2016, p. 19). In case of absence of such damages and losses at the household levels, the report says the GDP volume would be up by an average of 0.30 percent per year.

As far as food security in the postdisaster Bangladesh is concerned, mostly the poor and victims of natural disasters become the beneficiaries of the distribution of food grains under the PFDS. In Bangladesh, the Humanitarian Assistance Programme Implementation Guidelines 2012–2013 are in force for postdisaster crisis management and relief distribution. "An estimated 2.8 million tons of grain were distributed in 2012-13 (1.7 million tons of rice and 1.05 million tons of wheat) under monetized and non-monetized social safety net programs (SSNP)" (Ministry of Food, Government of Bangladesh 2015, p. 2). Nevertheless, according to the IFPRI, Bangladesh's high-poverty and undernutrition rates are exacerbated by frequent natural disasters and a high population density,

Table 7.4 Yearwise distribution of disaster-affected population in West Bengal and the available assessment of damages 2009–2017

Dates of incessant rains/ cyclone with tidal surge causing flood	Population affected	No. of human lives lost	No. of villages affected	No. of municipality/ ward affected	Crop area affected (in ha)	Estimated value of damaged crop (Rs in lakhs)	Total loss (Rs in crores)	Sources of data (assessment reports)
May 24, 2009-May 25, 2009 Aila cyclone and tidal surge	2,294,636(in 7 districts)	35	9,149	28	—	—	—	ReliefWeb
August 16, 2009–August 24, 2009	202,380(in 5 districts)	12	391	2	1,243	900	76.54 crore	ReliefWeb situation report
June 16, 2011	671,952(in 9 districts)	6	—	—	—	760 (only in Bankura district)	—	Sphere India (2011), Oxfam, and Save the Children
August 23, 2013–August 30, 2013	2,100,000(in 6 districts)	17	8,790	—	—	—	—	WBDM&CD portal
From mid-July 2015–July 30, 2015 (Cyclone Komen)	10,600,000(in 14 districts)	125	21,885	55	1,292,372	—	3,000crore	Sphere India (2015)
July 21, 2017–July 25, 2017	2,717,571(in 9 districts)	63	—	—	422,752.00	—	3,326.21 crore(Not fully assessed)	WB State Interagency Group an WBDM&CD (2017)
Total	18,586,539	258	40,215	85	1,716,367	1,660	6,402.75Crore	

Source: Different reports have been compiled.

and more than 17 percent of the total population (160 million) are still extremely poor (IFPRI 2018).

However, the assessment of the IFPRI (2016) regarding the flood impact reveals different views. On the basis of evaluation of "both household coping mechanisms and recovery rates in addition to examining how effectively national food distribution programs targeted food aid to those in greatest need" (IFPRI 2016, p. 11), the IFPRI (2016) came to the conclusion that in Bangladesh (i) poorest people cope with the floods by taking loans from private bank; (ii) although 53 policy advisory memos were produced by the Food Planning and Monitoring Unit of the Ministry of Food and Disaster Management between 1998 and 2001, these memos "needed to respond to the impacts of the flooding"; and (iii) import of huge quantity of rice in the private sector stabilized food market and prevented famine (p. 12). The highlights reveal that PFDS does not work effectively in postdisaster situation in Bangladesh, although Bangladesh has designed and approved the National Food Policy (2006) and the National Food Policy Plan of Action (2008–2015). It should be mentioned in this context that nowadays, in Bangladesh, the government gives more emphasis on the Vulnerable Group Development Programme in place of the Vulnerable Group Feeding Programme.

In India, the PDS has been operative since 1939, when war time rationing was introduced in Bombay and consequently to other cities in India. Since the 1970s especially since the *Garibi Hatao* program launched by former Indian Prime Minister Indira Gandhi in 1971 as antipoverty measures, the PDS through fair price ration shops became widely entrenched. But criticisms were leveled against the PDS because of its failure to serve the below-poverty-line (BPL) population, its urban bias, lack of transparency in delivering services, and poor coverage in the states with the highest rural population (Planning Commission, Government of India 2002, p. 368). So, for streamlining the system, the government issued special cards to BPL families and began selling food grains under the PDS to them at specially subsidized prices with effect from June 1997. Thus, the TPDS was initiated for making provision only for the BPL population for whom the allotment of food grains also increased at 50 percent of economic cost from 1 April 2000 (Planning Commission, Government of India 2002, p. 368). Later the National Food Security Act (NFSA) was passed in India in 2013, which ensures "access to adequate quantity of quality food at affordable prices to people to live a life with dignity." Thus, the NFSA wants to protect all children, women, and men in India including the vulnerable section of population from hunger and food deprivation. The act has detailed the TPDS as "the system for distribution of essential commodities to the ration card holders through fair price shops" and has made enough provisions for reform to deliver the food grains at the doorsteps of the priority people, to give preference to public institutions or public bodies such as panchayats, self-help groups, cooperatives, licensing of fair price shops, management of fair price shops by women or their collectives, and support to instituting grain banks. Yet, the method of identification of the priority people under the TPDS has been left to the state governments; in West Bengal, that is determined by the criteria of remaining below the poverty line.

The objectives of the PDS in West Bengal are to focus on providing food security to the people, particularly, the poor and vulnerable sections of the society. For maintaining the effective distribution of commodities, the PDS in West Bengal has been divided into two areas: (i) Urban Public Distribution System for municipalities and municipal corporations; and (ii) the PDS for other areas. The NFSA 2013 has been implemented in West Bengal since February 2016, and since then the beneficiaries have been classified as AAY households, priority household (PHH), and priority household with sugar (SPHH). Moreover, from February 1, 2016, the Rajya Khadya Suraksha Yojana (RKSY or State Food Security Programme) I and II have been initiated to cover all other people (RKSY II is for above-poverty-line [APL] people). Besides, Annapurna beneficiaries (from BPL people) holding special ration cards get 10 kg of rice per month free of cost.

From Table 7.5, it is clear that out of the total population of 91,276,115 in West Bengal, 85,903,464 are covered by the PDS, which is 94.11 percent of the total population. However, among this population, Non-NFSA RKSY II beneficiaries are from the APL population, which is 15.25 percent of the total population. The World Bank (2017) has mentioned the poverty level in West Bengal is 20 percent of the total population on the basis of 2012 BPL estimation, which is close to the national average of 19 percent. On this basis, one may come to the conclusion that food security implementation through the PDS is quite high in West Bengal.

Table 7.5 Beneficiaries of PDS in West Bengal (July 3, 2018)

State	AAY beneficiaries	NFSAPHH beneficiaries	NFSASPHH beneficiaries	Total NFSA beneficiaries (AAY + PHH + SPHH)	Non-NFSARKSYI beneficiaries	Non-NFSARKSYII beneficiaries	Total Non-NFSA (RKSYIRKSYII) beneficiaries
West Bengal	5,498,411	27,494,912	27,188,941	60,182,264	11,806,045	13,915,155	25,721,200

Source: Department of Food and Supplies, Government of West Bengal (2018).

Despite this positive picture, there are certain gray areas. The National Council of Applied Economic Research (NCAER), on the request of the Department of Food and Public Distribution of the Government of India, conducted a survey of the TPDS in six states in 2015. Three states—Bihar, Chhattisgarh, and Karnataka—implemented the NFSA, whereas West Bengal, Uttar Pradesh, and Assam did not implement NFSA at that time and were following the earlier TPDS. The NCAER attempted to assess whether the past weaknesses of the TPDS were adequately addressed by the six state governments or not. Report specified that although the network of PDS is strong in West Bengal, the average monthly take-home of food grain from PDS per BPL/PHH cardholder household per month in Bihar (4.49 kg) and West Bengal (5.96 kg) is substantially less than that in Assam (29.23 kg), Chhattisgarh (33.81 kg), Karnataka (27.11 kg), and Uttar Pradesh (32.6 kg).

Findings

From the above discussion, it is revealed that in both Bangladesh and West Bengal the PDS has evolved from food grain distribution through fair price ration shops to targeted distribution of food grains for vulnerable sections of the population. In West Bengal, there are BPL cards; likewise in Bangladesh, Vulnerable Group Feeding (VGF) cards are available for the extremely poor and flood-affected people. According to the International Labor Organization Social Security Portal regarding

Bangladesh (accessed June 25, 2018), from January 1, 2010 through December 31, 2010, an amount of 10,972 million taka was spent for VGF. Such scheme corresponds to AAY in West Bengal. Besides, in Bangladesh, there are two other programs under the PFDS: (i) test relief program, which ensures food for work or cash for work, and (ii) gratuitous relief for disaster-affected people. Cash-for-work program in postflood situations also leads to significant gains in the nutritional status of both children aged less than 5 years and women (Mascie-Taylor et al. 2010). In West Bengal, other than AAY, other PDS schemes are NFSA PHH, NFSA SPHH, Non-NFSA RKSYI, and Non-NFSA RKSYII, which provide coverage of more than 90 percent of the total population (Table 7.5). Besides, a huge number of farmers are covered by insurance schemes in West Bengal against the loss of crop due to flood or drought. In India, the National Rural Employment Guarantee Act 2005 ensures "livelihood security of the households in rural areas of the country by providing at least one hundred days of guaranteed wage employment in every financial year to every household." Thus, on the one hand, a strong PDS network and the insurance coverage of the loss of crop due to flood have made food security for the vulnerable population in West Bengal a reality. On the other hand, the insurance coverage is poor in Bangladesh. So the dependence of the poor solely on the PFDS in times of flood is quite natural.

In Bangladesh as well as in India, government data show that the PDS is well established with providing food security to substantial population. Nevertheless, the IFPRI revealed that flood-affected people in Bangladesh take private loans more to cope with flood than rely on the PFDS and also the policy memos for the PDS although are adopted, and are not implemented in a postflood situation. In case of West Bengal, the NCAER data also reveals that although the number of beneficiaries is very high in West Bengal, their take-home-per-household-per-month food grain quantity is very low. So, in both the countries there is a discrepancy regarding the PDS between government record and nongovernment assessment.

The leakage is a major issue in any of the PDS. But NCAER report (p. xvii) shows that in West Bengal leakage percentage was as high as 28.19 percent in 2015. Thus, the PDS in West Bengal suffers from large leakages, and the food grains targeted for the BPL people often go to the open market during transportation to and from fair price ration shops.

This is very important because India has the largest network of the PDS. In postdisaster situations, such leakage tends to be higher and may lead to politics of relief.

Conclusion

This chapter started with three research questions with regard to West Bengal and Bangladesh about (i) the existence of a sustainable PDS network in a postflood situation, (ii) the effectiveness of such PDS in ensuring food security in postflood situation, and (iii) any more requirements to make PDS more effective. The above exploration leads to the conclusion that both in Bangladesh and in West Bengal, PDS network is quite large and well established. However, there is some lacuna of these networks (mentioned earlier), which should be rectified. Because there is a dearth of analytical disaster census data relating food security status in postflood situation, it is difficult to specify the extent to which the PDS in these two countries may ensure food security in a postflood situation, especially after the first phase of the crisis is over. Yet, in both countries, emergency distribution of food grains following natural calamities for the vulnerable sections has been underscored.

To make the PDS more effective, first, comprehensive data regarding food security containing details about loss of workdays, damage to crops and crop area, impact on livelihood, insurance, relief and compensation amount, immigration after disaster in the postflood situation is required. Second, as in the case of maternity benefits, the National Food Security Act 2013 in India should have a provision on the benefits for disaster-affected people. In Bangladesh, PFDS guidelines mention the provision for disaster-hit people. Finally, to cope with the leakage, private operators in the PDS should not be engaged. In West Bengal, cooperatives, panchayats, or self-help groups may be entrusted with the responsibility of handling the PDS, for which provision has already been made in the National Food Security Act 2013. Sincere attempt to initiate these reforms may ensure the four pillars of food security—availability, access, utilization, and stability—in a transparent and efficient manner in both Bangladesh and West Bengal in a postflood situation.

References

Ahmad, Md. A. 2018. "Disaster Law and Community Resilience in Bangladesh." In *Disaster Law Emerging Thresholds*, ed. A. Singh. New York, NY: Routledge, pp. 80–95.

Ali, A.M.M.S., I. Jahan, A.R. Ahmed, and S. Rashid. 2008. "Public Food Distribution System in Bangladesh: Successful Reforms and Remaining Challenges." In *From Parastatals to Private Trade: Lessons from Asian Agriculture*, eds. S. Rashid, A. Gulati, and R. Cummings, Jr. Baltimore, MA: Johns Hopkins University, p. 115 (pp. 103–34).

Banu, N. 2015. "Chap. 2, Disaster Management in the Five Year Plans of Bangladesh: An Assessment." In *Strategic Disaster Risk Management in Asia,* eds. H. Ha, R.L.S. Fernando, and A. Mahmood. New Delhi: Springer, pp. 15–28.

BBS [Bangladesh Bureau of Statistics], 26.06.2016. 'Bangladesh Disaster-related Statistics, 2015 – Climate Change and Natural Disaster Perspectives' (presented by Md. R. Islam, Programme Director, Impact of Climate Change on Human Life): http://203 .112.218.65:8008/WebTestApplication/userfiles/Image/National %20Account%20Wing/Disaster_Climate/Presentation_Realease_ Climate15.pdf (accessed 10.3.2018).

Bhattacharyya, R. 2015. "Chap. 9, Administrative Planning and Political Response to a Post-Disaster Reconstruction: A Study of Aila (Cyclone)-Devastated Gosaba Block in West Bengal (India)." In *Strategic Disaster Risk Management in Asia*, eds. H. Ha, R.L.S. Fernando, and A. Mahmood. New Delhi: Springer, pp. 115–28.

Bhattacharyya, R. 2018. "Can Laws Ensure Disaster Risk Reduction? A Study of Mandarmani Sea Beach in West Bengal." In *Disaster Law Emerging Thresholds*, ed. A. Singh. New York, NY: Routledge, pp. 345–58.

Chakraborty, D., S. Bandyopadhyay, I. Dasgupta, S. Sen, and D. Mitra. 2013. "Chap. 9, Natural Disaster Mitigation in West Bengal." In *The Economic Impacts of Natural Disasters*, eds. D. Guha-Sapir, and I. Santos. New York, NY: Oxford, pp. 199–225.

Flanagan, B.E., E.W. Gregory, E.J. Hallisey, J.L. Heitgerd, and B. Lewis. 2011. "A Social Vulnerability Index for Disaster Management."

Journal of Homeland Security and Emergency Management 8, no. 1, Article 3.

Maitra, H, 2018. "Disaster Governance in West Bengal, India." In *Disaster Risk Governance in India and Cross Cutting Issues*, eds. I. Pal, and R. Shaw. Singapore: Springer, pp. 105–26.

Ozaki, M. 2016. "Disaster Risk Financing in Bangladesh." ADB South Asia Working Paper Series, No. 46, Manila: ADB.

Pal, I., and T. Ghosh. 2018. "Risk Governance Measures and Actions in Sundarbans Delta (India): A Holistic Analysis of Post-disaster Situations of Cyclone Aila." In *Disaster Risk Governance in India and Cross Cutting Issues*, eds. I. Pal, and R. Shaw. Singapore: Springer, pp. 225–42.

Parvin, G.A., K. Fujita, A. Matsuyama, R. Shaw, and M. Sakamoto. 2015. "Chapter 13, Climate Change, Flood, Food Security and Human Health: Cross-Cutting Issues in Bangladesh." In *Food Security and Risk Reduction in Bangladesh,* eds. U. Habiba, Md. A. Abedin, A.W.R. Hassan, and R. Shaw. Tokyo: Springer, pp. 235–54.

Planning Commission, Government of India. 2002. "Chapters 3 and 4, Public Distribution System." *Tenth Five Year Plan—2002–2007 Sectoral Policies and Programmes,* Vol. 2. New Delhi: Planning Commission, Government of India, pp. 365–79.

Radhakrishna, R., and K. Subbarao. 1997. *India's Public Distribution System A National and International Perspective.* World Bank Discussion Paper No. 380, World Bank, Washington, DC.

Schendel, W.V. 2009. *A History of Bangladesh.* Cambridge, UK: Cambridge University Press.

Wisner, B., P. Blaikie, T. Cannon, and I. Davis. 2004. *At Risk, Natural Hazards, People's Vulnerability and Disasters.* London, UK: Routledge.

World Bank. 2013. *Bangladesh Poverty Assessment—Assessing a Decade of Progress in Reducing Poverty 2000–2010.* Chapters 7 and 8, Bangladesh Development Series, Paper No. 31. Dhaka: World Bank, pp. 94–120.

Internet Sources

Asian Development Bank. 2016. "Disaster Risk Financing in Bangladesh." Manila: ADB. https://www.adb.org/sites/default/files/publication/198561/sawp-046.pdf (accessed May 25, 2018).

Balani, S. December, 2013. "Functioning of the Public Distribution System An Analytical Report." PRS Legislative Research, p. 2. http://www.prsindia .org/administrator/uploads/general/1388728622~~TPDS%20 Thematic%20Note.pdf. Accessed January 31, 2018.

Bangladesh Bureau of Statistics. June, 2016. "Bangladesh Disaster-related Statistics, 2015—Climate Change and Natural Disaster Perspectives" (presented by Md. R. Islam, Programme Director, Impact of Climate Change on Human Life): http://203.112.218.65:8008/WebTestApplication/ userfiles/Image/National%20Account%20Wing/Disaster_Climate/ Presentation_Realease_Climate15.pdf (accessed March 10, 2018).

Bengal Chamber of Commerce. 2013. "Government of West Bengal Executive Summary of State Economic Review." http://www.bengalchamber .com/economic-indicators.html (accessed March 15, 2018).

Department of Food and Supplies, Government of West Bengal. 2018. https://202.61.117.98/RCCount_District.aspx (accessed June 20, 2018).

Food and Agricultural Organization of the United Nations. 2015. *The Impact of Natural Hazards and Disasters on Agriculture and Food Security and Nutrition. A Call for Action to Build Resilient Livelihoods*, p. 3. http://www.fao.org/3/a-i4434e.pdf (accessed May 16, 2018).

Government of India, Ministry of Agriculture and Farmers Welfare. 2017. "Compensation for Damaged Crops under Insurance Scheme." Lok Sabha Unstarred Question No. 2026. Annexure – I http://www .indiaenvironmentportal.org.in/files/file/Compensation%20for%20 Damaged%20Crops%20under%20Insurance%20Scheme.pdf (accessed May 25, 2018).

IFPRI, P. Menon, A. Deolalikar, and A. Bhaskar. 2009. "India State Hunger Index Comparisons of Hunger Across States." http://ebrary.ifpri.org/ cdm/ref/collection/p15738coll2/id/13891 (accessed May 31, 2018).

International Food Policy Research Institute. 2016. "Highlights of Recent IFPRI Research and Partnerships in Bangladesh: Reducing Poverty and Hunger through Food Policy Research." https://www.ifpri .org/publication/highlights-recent-ifpri-research-and-partnerships- bangladesh (accessed May 16, 2018).

International Food Policy Research Institute. 2017. *Global Hunger Index: The Inequalities of Hunger,* Washington DC: IFPRI, p. 13. http://www .globalhungerindex.org/pdf/en/2017.pdf (accessed May 25, 2018).

International Food Policy Research Institute. 2018. Food Security Portal. "Country Resources: Bangladesh." http://www.foodsecurityportal .org/bangladesh/resources (accessed May 25, 2018).

International Labour Organization, Social Security Department, Bangladesh. http://www.ilo.org/dyn/ilossi/ssimain.updSchemeExpenditure? p_lang=en&p_geoaid=50&p_scheme_id=1356&p_social_ id=2314 (accessed June 25, 2018).

Mascie-Taylor, C.G.N., M.K. Marks, R. Goto, and R. Islam. 2010. "Impact of a Cash-for-work Programme on Food Consumption and Nutrition among Women and Children Facing Food Insecurity in Rural Bangladesh." *Bulletin of the World Health Organization* 88, 854–60. http://www.who.int/bulletin/volumes/88/11/10-080994/en (accessed June 25, 2018).

Ministry of Food, Government of Bangladesh. http://www.dgfood.gov .bd (accessed May, 2018).

Ministry of Food, Government of Bangladesh. 2015. "Terms of Reference for Integrated Food Policy Research Program" under Modern Food Storage Facilities Project. http://dgfood.portal.gov.bd/sites/ default/files/files/dgfood.portal.gov.bd/page/cb9f6c96_eeef_486e_ adb9_c7b3e786f761/Final%20TOR%20for%20Integrated%20 Research%20Program-08-06-01-15.pdf (accessed May 20, 2018).

Ministry of Statistics and Programme Implementation, Government of India. http://www.mospi.gov.in (accessed May, 2018).

National Disaster Management Authority of India. https://ndma.gov.in/ en (accessed May, 2018).

National Food Policy 2006, 14 August, 2006. Ministry of Food and Disaster Management, Dhaka, Government of Bangladesh https:// extranet.who.int/nutrition/gina/sites/default/files/BGD%202006% 20National%20food%20policy.pdf (accessed May 18 2018)

'National Food Policy Plan of Action (2008-2015)' 5 August, 2008. Food Planning and Monitoring Unit (FPMU), Ministry of Food and Disaster Management, Dhaka, Government of Bangladesh. https:// www.gafspfund.org/sites/default/files/inline-files/NationalFood PolicyPlanofActionFINAL.pdf (accessed May 20, 2018)

The National Council of Applied Economic Research. 2015. "Evaluation Study of Targeted Public Distribution System in Selected States." p. xv.

http://dfpd.nic.in/writereaddata/images/TPDS-140316.pdf (accessed May 20, 2018).

NITI Aayog Development Monitoring and Evaluation Office, Government of India. 2016. "Evaluation Study on Role of Public Distribution System in Shaping Household and Nutritional Security India." Development Monitoring and Evaluation Office Report No. 233. http://niti.gov.in/writereaddata/files/document_publication/Final%20PDS%20Report-new.pdf (accessed June 14,2018).

Oxfam and Save the Children. 2011."Rapid Assessment Report—Floods and Heavy Downpour in West Bengal, India." http://www.sphereindia.org.in/Download/Rapid%20 Assessment%20Report%20WB%20Flood%20(oxfam%20&%20SCBR).pdf (accessed May 25, 2018).

Prasad, E., and N. Mukherjee. 2014. "Situation Analysis on Floods and Flood Management." International Union for Conservation of Nature and Natural Resources (IUCN), Gland, Switzerland. https://cmsdata.iucn.org/downloads/situation_analysis_on_floods.pdf (accessed May 16, 2018).

Public Distribution System, Govt. of West Bengal. https://wbpds.gov.in (accessed May, 2018).

ReliefWeb. 2009. "Situation Report West Bengal Floods." https://reliefweb.int/sites/reliefweb.int/files/resources/ED5E08CD-25802034C125761F00469C70-Full_Report.pdf (accessed May 25, 2018).

Sphere India. 2011. "Joint Flood Assessment Report West Bengal." http://www.sphereindia.org.in/Download/Joint%20Flood%20Assessment%20Report%20(bankura%20&%20E-medinipur).pdf (accessed May 25, 2018).

Sphere India. 2015. "Joint Needs Assessment Report West Bengal Floods." https://reliefweb.int/sites/reliefweb.int/files/resources/west-bengal-jna-report-august-2015_30-08-2015.pdf (accessed May 25, 2018).

Tapsell, S., S. McCarthy, H. Faulkner, and M. Alexander. 2010. "Social Vulnerability and Natural Hazards. CapHaz-Net WP4 Report." Flood Hazard Research Centre—FHRC, Middlesex University, London. http://caphaz-net.org/outcomes-results/CapHaz-Net_WP4_Social-Vulnerability.pdf (accessed April 25, 2018).

West Bengal Disaster Management Authority. http://wbdmd.gov.in (accessed May, 2018).

West Bengal State Inter Agency Group in Collaboration with Department of Disaster Management, Government of West Bengal. 2017. "Report of Joint Rapid Need Assessment South Bengal Flood 2017." https://reliefweb.int/sites/reliefweb.int/files/resources/jrna-report-of-south-bengal-flood-2017.pdf (accessed May 25, 2018).

World Bank. 2013. Bangladesh Poverty Assessment: Assessing a Decade of Progress in Reducing Poverty, 2000-2010 [Bangladesh Development Series Paper No. 31], World Bank, Dhaka. http://documents.worldbank.org/curated/en/109051468203350011/pdf/785590NWP0Bang00Box0377348B0PUBLIC0.pdf (accessed May 25, 2018)

World Bank. 2017. "West Bengal Poverty, Growth & Inequality." http://documents.worldbank.org/curated/en/315791504252302097/pdf/119344-BRI-P157572-West-Bengal-Poverty.pdf (accessed May 25, 2018).

CHAPTER 8

Urban Flooding and Threats to Sustainable Development: A Study of Srinagar and Chennai Floods

Himanshu Shekhar Mishra

New Delhi Television, India

Introduction

The rise in the scale and frequency of natural disasters is increasingly threatening human life, private and public properties, and the development processes in disaster-prone zones of the world. What is more alarming is the gradual increase in climate and weather-related disaster events. A joint study by the United Nations Office for Disaster Risk Reduction (UNISDR) and the Centre for Research on the Epidemiology of Disasters (CRED) has found that the frequency of climate- and weather-related disasters have risen significantly in the last two decades. Between 1976 and 1995, a total of 3,017 such disaster incidents were recorded. However, over the next two decades (1996-2015), the number of recorded climate- and weather-related disaster incidents more than doubled to 6,392 (UNISDR and CRED 2016). In fact, a separate study has cited the data available with Emergency Events Database (EM-DAT) to argue that the number of climate-related disaster has risen by 44 percent since 2000 on an annual basis in comparison with the 1994-2000 average (UNISDR and CRED 2015).

The high degree of threat posed by natural disasters is evident from the fact that in the first semester of 2017 alone, a total of 149 disasters occurred in 73 countries, which killed 3,162 people, affected lives of more than 80 million people, and caused an economic loss of US$32.4-billion (CRED Crunch 2017). Natural disasters are also leading to large-scale internal displacements, forcing millions of poor and the underprivileged people every year worldwide to leave their traditional homeland and meager sources of livelihood to safer locales to survive the wrath of nature. In its "Global Report on Internal Displacement," the Internal Displacement Monitoring Centre (2017) of the Norwegian Refugee Council argued that natural disasters displaced 24.2 million people in 2016 alone at the global level. The data available with Norwegian Refugee Council shows that a total of 227.6 million people were displaced between 2008 and 2017 (Internal Displacement Monitoring Centre 2017). What is more worrisome is that natural disasters are increasingly causing large-scale economic losses at the global level. The leading insurance and risk management company Aon Benfield has claimed that natural disasters caused a total economic loss of US$210 billion in 2016. This is 21 percent more than the average economic losses caused by natural disasters over the last 16 years (Benfield 2016).

India is one of the worst natural disaster–affected countries in the world. It lost 97,691 lives in natural disasters between 1996 and 2015 (UNISDR and CRED 2016). In terms of the number of people affected, India was the worst natural disaster–affected country in the world, with 17 natural disasters affecting the lives of more than 330 million people in 2016 (Guha-Sapiret et al. 2016). In fact, the most disturbing is the rise in the frequency of flood disasters in India. Between 1996 and 2005, 13,660 lives were lost in 67 flood incidents but in the subsequent decade (2006-2015), a total of 15,860 lost their lives in 90 flood incidents (UNISDR and CRED 2016).

This chapter attempts to assess the impact of natural disasters on sustainable development in India. It is based on a study of two of the most severe natural disasters in recent years: the devastating floods in Jammu and Kashmir in September 2014 and the unprecedented floods in Chennai 14 months later in November–December 2015. Based on the empirical data accessed from government agencies, the United Nations, and independent research institutions, it attempts to show how natural disasters are gradually threatening the sustainable development processes in India. It also critically tries to assess the weaknesses in India's disaster management framework and how loopholes in India's disaster preparedness especially in urban areas have made its important cities more vulnerable to fight the threat posed by natural disasters.

Review of Documents

The devastating Tsunami in December 2004 changed the contours of the global discourse on natural disasters. It forced the nations to review their disaster management strategies and formulate a legislative response to combat the challenge posed by natural disasters. Indian Parliament passed a legislation titled *Disaster Management Act* in December 2005, which laid a politico-legal framework at the national level with a three-tier disaster response structure to strengthen India's disaster management machinery. Five years later, in 2009, the National Policy on Disaster Management was also formulated.

This chapter attempts to critically study the *Disaster Management Act 2005*, the National Policy on Disaster Management (2009), the National Disaster Management Plan (2016), the research and policy documents available with the Ministry of Home Affairs, NDMA and the National Institute of Disaster Management (NIDM) on Jammu and Kashmir and Chennai floods, official reports of the Parliamentary Standing Committee on Home Affairs and Water Resources and official records of debates in both the Houses of Indian Parliament. An attempt has also been made to critically analyze the empirical studies by global institutions like the UNISDR and the CRED, the Emergency Events Database (EM-DAT), the Internal Displacement Monitoring Centre of the Norwegian Refugee Council, and the Aon Benfield Analytics.

Objectives of the Study

This chapter attempts to assess the devastating impact of natural disasters on life, public and private properties, and the economy in a given disaster-affected region; the lessons they pose for the future; and how they make it imperative for India to formulate sustainable development strategies and restructure its legislative and administrative response to natural disasters. It is an empirical effort to study the impact of natural disasters on sustainable development processes in India. It is based on a study of two natural disasters: the severe floods in Jammu and Kashmir in September 2014 and the unprecedented floods in Chennai 14 months later in November–December 2015. It argues for an urgent need to integrate a disaster risk management vision within India's overall sustainable development strategy. It also calls for aligning India's sustainable development policies with the global sustainable development targets set by the United Nations as outlined in the Sendai Framework 2015.

Research Methodology

The basic thrust of this chapter is to analytically study the impact of floods on the common people and economy in the affected zones in both Srinagar district and the Chennai metropolitan area. The basic empirical facts used in this chapter have been drawn from research documents available from the UNISDR, the CRED, Internal Displacement Monitoring Centre (Norwegian Refugee Council), and the official reports submitted to the Parliament of India by Parliamentary Standing Committee on Home Affairs and Water Resources on the postdisaster reconstruction and rehabilitation work in disaster-hit zones in Jammu and Kashmir and Chennai.

The official documents prepared by the Ministry of Home Affairs and the Jammu and Kashmir and Tamil Nadu state governments; reports released by reinsurance agency Aon Benfield Analytics; official documents accessed from the NDMA; and the National Disaster Relief Force (NDRF) have also been critically studied and analyzed. Information and facts collected as a news correspondent during the devastating floods in Srinagar and adjoining areas and interviews with the flood-affected people in different parts of Srinagar city, senior law makers, and government officials directly involved with relief and rescue work in Jammu and Kashmir have also been included in this chapter. This chapter is an attempt to analyze and collate empirical facts to highlight the growing threat posed by natural disasters to India's important urban centers and highlight the gaps in the existing legislative and policy framework to deal with natural disasters in India.

The Jammu and Kashmir Floods: The Worst Since 1902

The devastating floods in Jammu and Kashmir in September 2014 exposed the chinks in India's disaster management framework, especially in important urban centers. As large parts of Srinagar city and adjoining urban areas went under water, it raised fundamental questions on the ability of India's important cities to face natural disasters of such high intensity and scale. Considered the worst flood to hit the picturesque valley since 1902, it exposed the gaps that existed in the implementation of basic legislative provisions as outlined in the *Disaster Management Act 2005*. Large parts of Srinagar and adjoining districts remained submerged in flood waters for more than 3 weeks. It followed above-average rainfall in 10 out of 22 districts of the state. The recorded rainfall was highest in Shopian district, which received 2,953 percent above normal rainfall while the Srinagar district received 1,410 percent above normal rainfall (Rajya Sabha Secretariat Report 2014).

The failure of the meteorological department to alert the state agencies in advance about the impending danger from abnormally high-level of rainfall further exacerbated the flood crises. The official state machinery was caught off-guard in the absence of any actionable warning (Venugopal and Yasir 2017). Per official data, 254,000 houses were fully or partially damaged in the floods and at least 287 people lost their lives (Rajya Sabha Secretariat 2014). The scale of devastation was so high that it turned out to be the worst natural disaster of the world in 2014 in terms of the economic loss it caused. According to the Annual Disaster Statistical Review 2014 conducted by CRED, Institute of Health and Society, and the Université Catholique de Louvain, it cost India up to US$16-billion in economic losses (Guha-Sapiret, Hoyois, and Below 2014).

The failure of the meteorological department to issue any actionable warning gave little time to the local populace and tourists to take precautionary measures and move to safer locations (Mittal 2017). The huge devastation caused by floods was visible everywhere, that is, almost all major hospitals in Srinagar city remained submerged in flood water for days incapacitating the health infrastructure in the city. Landslides in hilly areas destroyed highways at several locations, making it difficult for disaster relief agencies to evacuate people and carry relief material to the disaster-affected zones by road route. Hundreds of communication towers had collapsed disrupting mobile and communication services in the valley and thus seriously affecting the ability of affected populace to seek help from relief and rescue agencies.

The flood crisis was aggravated by the fact that the state government had not even constituted a state disaster response force 9 years after the *Disaster Management Act* made it mandatory in 2005 for all states to constitute such a force. As the state government watched helplessly, the flood crises unfolded in India's strategically most important border state, submerging important installations in flood waters for several days. This made it difficult for relief agencies to provide basic civic amenities to the flood-affected populace. As the public healthcare system collapsed, the fear of an epidemic loomed large. The dead bodies of animals were seen openly floating along the banks of Jhelum River. The impact on the state economy was so huge that it shrunk the income of the state government by 1.5 percent in 2014–2015 (Government of Jammu and Kashmir 2015–2016).

What Caused Floods in Jammu and Kashmir?

The official documents show that Jammu and Kashmir state government did not act seriously on specific warnings and alerts issued by leading state agencies. The NIDM, India's premier institution dealing with disaster research, had categorically warned the Jammu and Kashmir government 2 years back in 2012 that illegal and unauthorized construction on river banks in the state was destroying the river ecosystem. NIDM had specifically cautioned that "Sand and gravel dredging or top soil denudation for brick industry to support growing real estate industry have significantly enhanced the human induced disaster risk in the eco-sensitive zones of the State" (J&K ENVIS Centre 2016). But as the flood tragedy unfolded in the valley, it became clear that the state government had failed to act seriously on such warnings.

In fact, the state government not only failed to undertake disaster mitigation measures and stop illegal construction and encroachment of river banks, it also made no concerted effort to sensitize people living along river banks to the danger that floods posed to their lives and property. In many inundated areas, the flood victims could be seen living in open make-shift tents along the river bed as dead bodies of animals flowed in Jhelum River just a few meters away. Many flood victims even refused to leave their flooded homes forcibly ignoring the warnings that it could endanger their lives. The failure of the civic agencies to maintain a viable drainage system in the city aggravated the flood crisis. It forced hundreds of thousands of people to seek shelter in relief camps and make-shift homes as their homes remained submerged in flood waters for more than a week. The Centre for Science and Environment (CSE) has termed the collapse of the drainage system in Srinagar city as the primary reason behind the heavy damage caused by floods. In its investigative report, the CSE has argued that between 1911 and 2004, Srinagar city lost half of its water bodies. The unplanned urbanization has led to encroachment of lakes, which has reduced their ability to absorb water during floods (Narain 2016).

Chennai Floods (November–December 2015)

Flood waters returned to haunt India again 14 months later when large parts of Chennai, the capital city of Tamil Nadu, and a few adjoining districts faced unprecedented deluge. It followed unprecedented heavy rainfall during the annual northeast monsoon, affecting a large part of the Coromandel Coast region of Southern India, especially the Chennai cosmopolitan region. The Tamil Nadu government informed the Parliamentary Standing Committee on Home Affairs that Chennai City was the worst affected in the deluge. It is estimated that 470 people died, more than 12,000 cattle were killed, 492,000 houses were damaged or destroyed, and hundreds of thousands of people were displaced (Rajya Sabha Secretariat 2016).

Considered the worst urban flood in the history of this important metropolitan city, it highlighted the dangers that natural disasters posed to India's important urban centers. It severely disrupted economic activity in the industrial zone, brought to a standstill thousands of big and small industrial units in the Chennai metropolitan area. The flood crisis was exacerbated by encroachments in lakes and river channels and also congestion in Chennai city's drainage system. In its report tabled in Parliament on the Chennai floods, the Parliamentary Standing Committee on Home Affairs has argued that encroachments have significantly reduced the carrying capacity of water bodies. The failure of civic agencies to carry out de-silting of the storm water drains further exacerbated the problem in Chennai (Rajya Sabha Secretariat 2016). The problem was compounded by the failure of the civic agencies to act despite several warnings regarding the significant decline in the carrying capacity of water bodies in Chennai (Narayan 2018).

The state administration estimated that floods had affected industrial operations in more than 165 BSE-listed companies collectively worth over 285,000 crore rupees (1 crore is 10 million). Large number of multinational corporations were forced to shut their production line during these floods. It included multinational companies such as Hyundai, Ford, BMW, Nissan, TVS, Renault-Nissan, and Ashok Leyland (Express News Service 2015). The impact of floods was more severe on small- and medium-scale industries. The leading industry association ASSOCHAM estimated the losses at more than 15,000 crore rupees (ASSOCHAM 2015). The reinsurance agency Aon Benfield Analytics estimated the overall losses caused by floods at much higher at 20,000 crore rupees (approximately US\$3 billion) (Benfield 2015). The assessment of the loss calculated by the state government was much higher even though the economic assistance it received from the central government was much less. The Parliamentary Standing Committee on Home Affairs argues in its report tabled in Parliament:

The Ministry informed that in response to the demand of Tamil Nadu State Government for Rs. 25912.46 crore for relief, rehabilitation, rebuilding and restoration till the end of December, only Rs. 2195 crore was provided, which was one-fourth of the amount required for temporary relief projected by the State Government. (Rajya Sabha Secretariat 2016, p. 13)

Findings of the Study

These two flood incidents in two of India's important cities, separated by more than 3,000 kilometers, raised fundamental questions about the state of preparedness of India's important cities to face natural disasters. They exposed the fault lines in India's disaster management strategy and highlighted the vulnerability of urban India with regard to the threat posed by natural disasters. The heavy damages caused to human life and property by these two unprecedented flood incidents were largely because of the mushrooming of illegal colonies and housing structures along river beds in blatant violation of environmental norms and building by-laws and congestion in the city drainage systems. The encroachment of river bed by real estate mafia significantly reduced the water-carrying capacity of the Jhelum River in Srinagar and the important lakes in and around Chennai city. Absence of regular desilting operations and effective flood zone planning further compounded the problem during both the flood incidents.

Questions have also been raised about the failure of drainage systems in case of both Srinagar and Chennai floods and the neglect of natural water bodies by the local civic agencies. In its study of the water bodies in Chennai, the CSE cited the records available with the Water Resources Department of Tamil Nadu to highlight the problem of encroachment, which significantly reduced the storage capacity of major lakes and drains in the city. The official records show the area of 19 major lakes shrunk from 1,130 hectares in the 1980s to around 645 hectares by the early 2000s. It significantly reduced their storage capacity. The CSE research has also shown that storm water drains are clogged and required urgent attention (Narain 2016). Importantly, a Chennai Metropolitan Authority Report revealed that construction of 150,000 illegal structures destroyed around 300 water bodies in Chennai (Samuel, Annadurai, and Sankarakrishnan 2018).

In the wake of lessons thrown up by these two natural disasters, India needs to initiate urgent steps to reform its existing regulatory and legislative norms related to disaster management. To strengthen the legislative framework to combat natural disasters, it would be incumbent to incorporate new provisions in the existing *Disaster Management Act 2005* to give more powers to states and raise new battalions of National Disaster Response Forces to launch effective relief and rescue missions in disaster-affected zones. To combat the threat of an epidemic in a disaster-affected zone, it would also be necessary to raise a specialized National Disaster Medical Response Force, comprising trained doctors and para-medic staff, to provide immediate medical aid to affected people. India urgently needs to take these steps to strengthen the capabilities of govern-ment agencies to combat natural disasters in future, especially since India is a high disaster-prone country. The key focus should be centered on four important infrastructure sectors, namely, health, energy, transport, and telecommunication sectors because they are considered critical for launching effective relief measures and in initiating postdisaster recon-struction and rehabilitation work in disaster-affected zones. The delay in initiating steps toward strengthening the resilience of Indian cities could have serious ramification because it will increase their degree of vulner-ability to natural disasters (Kapucu and Liou 2014).

It is significant to note that important concepts like "sustainable develop-ment" and "insurance" do not even exist in the *Disaster Management Act 2005*. The National Policy on Disaster Management (2009) is silent on the idea of "compensation" to disaster victims. There are also questions on how far the states have implemented the mandatory provisions with regard to set-ting up important institutions like a State Disaster Response Force (SDRF). At the time of floods in Jammu and Kashmir, the SDRF had not been set up even 9 years after the *Disaster Management Act* made it mandatory in 2005.

A New Strategy for Urban Floods Disaster Management

The Government of India has taken the first step to address the serious challenge posed by urban floods. The National Disaster Management Plan (NDMP), officially released in May 2016, 5 months after the Chennai floods, has recommended a differential strategy to counter the threat posed by urban floods. The NDMP document calls for a separate "Urban Floods Disaster Management" strategy to strengthen the capabil-ity of Indian cities to combat natural disasters:

Urban flooding is significantly different from rural flooding as urbanization leads to developed catchments which increases the flood peaks from 1.8 to 8 times and flood volumes by up to

6 times. Consequently, flooding occurs very quickly due to "faster flow times," sometimes in a matter of minutes. (National Disaster Management Plan 2016, p. 22)

The rapid urbanization is posing a serious challenge for disaster management as it is pushing millions of Indians to migrate from rural to urban centers in search of education, employment, and better livelihood opportunities. The majority of migrants are unskilled and poor, and they cannot afford the high cost of living in main urban centers. The consequent mushrooming of illegal colonies to house this growing mass of migrant population is especially alarming in high disaster-prone zones (Mahajan and Mahajan 2015). To address this challenge, India needs to link the principle of sustainable development with its disaster risk reduction strategy and adopt an integrated approach to fight the threat posed by natural disasters (Uitto and Shaw 2016). At an International Workshop on Disaster Resilient Infrastructure, India's nodal agency dealing with natural disasters, the National Disaster Management Agency argued that India needed a total of US$1.5-trillion investment in the infrastructure sector over the next 10 years (National Disaster Management Authority 2018). This makes it imperative for India to urgently weave a disaster-resilient component in its overall development strategy to make its future urban infrastructure projects more sustainable and disaster resilient. The role of municipal and other civic agencies would be critical especially in flood-prone cities. They will have to take effective measures to strengthen the flood-control infrastructure and early warning systems, improve the network of storm sewers, and initiate steps toward climate risk management (Jha, Brechte, and Stanton-Geddes 2015).

This is especially significant considering that the existing norms in many vulnerable states do not adequately reflect the disaster-resilient component especially while building critical development infrastructure like dams and hydropower projects in high-seismic and flood-prone zones. For example, in seismically vulnerable state of Himachal Pradesh, which is located in seismic zone IV, researchers have found that detailed project reports related with construction of new dams do not adequately address the seismicity and other disaster-related risk elements (Mahajan and Mahajan 2015).

Government of India has initiated steps to address this challenge. Prime Minister Narendra Modi outlined a 10-point agenda at the Asian

Ministerial Conference on Disaster Risk Reduction (AMCDRR) 2016. It included incorporating a disaster risk reduction vision in India's economic development agenda, strengthening the risk coverage mechanism and initiate new measures toward disaster mitigation (Press Information Bureau 2016). He also emphasized the urgent need to strengthen the insurance culture among both the poor and the rich, small and medium enterprises to multinational corporations. In fact, the absence of an insurance culture in Kashmir and the Chennai region made it difficult for large number of individuals and small business units to seek claims for the economic losses they had suffered during the unprecedented floods. India also needs to involve the burgeoning private sector enterprises to effectively fight this challenge. They can play an important role especially in key infrastructure sectors like power generation where they have a significant presence (Sharma 2013).

Sendai Framework: A Global Roadmap on DRR

As India grapples with the challenge posed by natural disasters, it also needs to align its objectives and priorities with the global agenda on disaster risk reduction as outlined in the Sendai Framework. The Sendai Framework attempts to link disaster risk reduction with sustainable development initiatives and delineates the basis for a risk-informed and resilient sustainable global development agenda. It categorically makes it mandatory for small and big business enterprises to integrate disaster risk reduction practices in their management practices and enhance their investments in disaster risk reduction strategies (United Nations 2015, Section V, 36c). The Sendai Framework also sets a deadline for the global community to include disaster risk reduction component in urban planning processes, building codes and more investment in quake-resistant infrastructure (United Nations 2015).

The damages caused by Jammu and Kashmir and Chennai floods have made it imperative for India to undertake these measures as defined in the Sendai Framework and align its disaster management strategy with the global targets. At the Asian Ministerial Conference on Disaster Risk Reduction (AMCDRR) in Ulaanbaatar in Mongolia, the Indian representative underscored the importance of strengthening disaster-resilient infrastructure per the Sendai Framework recommendations. An official release issued by the Indian Home Ministry on AMCDRR categorically referred to this point:

> Dr P K Mishra, Additional Principal Secretary to the Prime Minister . . . emphasized that without mainstreaming of Disaster Risk Reduction in development it will be nearly impossible to achieve the loss reduction targets—in mortality, number of affected people, economic losses and infrastructure losses—enshrined in the Sendai Framework for Disaster Risk Reduction. (Ministry of Home Affairs 2018, p. 1)

Considering the growing cross-border threat posed by the natural disasters, India also needs to work with important regional groupings like SAARC and the BRICS and develop an institutional mechanism to strengthen regional and international cooperation in this regard. The initiatives undertaken by European nations in creating an integrated knowledge base related to regional hazards, identification and mapping of vulnerable areas, and shared disaster response mechanism is significant (Delmonaco 2011, p. 24). It would require special focus on capacity building and sensitization of the communities living in high disaster-risk zones. This would also require a high level of empathy and integrity to effectively implement these important social and policy measures on the ground (Sharma, Agrawal, and Bharti 2015, p. 151).

Conclusion: A Roadmap for Future

Both Srinagar and Chennai floods have exposed the vulnerability of India's major urban centers to combat natural disasters. At the larger level, they have highlighted the weaknesses in India's disaster management strategy. The rampant encroachment of lakes and illegal construction along river banks are increasingly threatening the resilience of Indian cities to fight natural disasters. The gradual rise in climate and weather-related disaster incidents makes it incumbent for India to initiate urgent steps to strengthen the existing legislative framework to deal with this threat at both national and state level, create new institutions like a National

Disaster Medical Response Force, strengthen the capability of existing institutions like National Disaster Response Force by raising new battalions, and launch effective disaster mitigation measures. India also needs to adopt a multidimensional approach by incorporating a disaster risk management vision in its urban development strategy to counter the rising threat of urban flooding.

References

Aon Benfield Analytics. November, 2016. *2016 Annual Global Climate and Catastrophe Report.* Aon Benfield Analytics. http://thoughtleadership.aonbenfield.com/Documents/20170117-ab-if-annual-climate-catastrophe-report.pdf

Associated Chambers of Commerce of India. December 02, 2015. "Financial Loss Due to Unprecedented Downpour in TN may Cross Rs 15K Crore". http://www.assocham.org/newsdetail.php?id=5362

Centre for Research on the Epidemiology of Disaster and UN Office for Disaster Risk Reduction. 2015. "The Human Cost of Natural Disasters: A Global Perspective."

Centre for Research on the Epidemiology of Disaster and UN Office for Disaster Risk Reduction. 2016. "Poverty & Death: Disaster Mortality, 1996–2015".

CRED Crunch. 2017. "Disaster Data: A Balanced Perspective". Issue No. 48, September. https://reliefweb.int/report/world/cred-crunch-newsletter-issue-no-48-september-2017-disaster-data-balanced-perspective

Delmonaco, G., F. Atun, A. Ceudech, H. Deeming, A. De Roo, D. Lumbroso, A. Galderisi, M. Kallache, J. P. Kropp, S. Kundak, D. Molinari, F. Tweed, S. Wade, G. Walker, M. Dandoulaki, and J. Barredo. 2011. Europe at risk (Following EU-funded research on hazard and risks). In *Inside Risk: A Strategy for Sustainable Risk Mitigation*, eds. S. Menoni, and C. Margottini. Milono, Italy: Springer-Verlag.

Government of Jammu and Kashmir. 2015–2016. Finance Minister Budget Speech.Guha-Sapir, D., P. Hoyois, and R. Below, eds. 2014. *Annual Disaster Statistical Review 2016, The Numbers and Trends.* Brussels: CRED. p. 2.

Guha-Sapir, D., P. Hoyois, P. Wallemacq, and R. Below, eds. 2016. *Annual Disaster Statistical Review 2016, The Numbers and Trends.* Brussels: CRED. p. 21.

Internal Displacement Monitoring Centre. 2017. *Global Report on Internal Displacement 2017.* Geneva, Switzerland: IDMC.

Jha, A., H. Brechte, and Z. Stanton-Geddes. 2015. "Building Resilience to Disasters and Climate Change in the Age of Urbanization". In *Disaster Risk Reduction for Economic Growth and Livelihood: Investing in Resilience and Development,* eds. I. Davis, K. Yanagisawa, and K. Georgieva. New York, NY: Routledge.

J&K ENVIS Centre. 2016. *Disaster.* Ministry of Environment & Forest, Government of India. http://jkenvis.org/disaster_introduction.html

Kapucu, N., and K.T. Liou. 2014. "Disasters and Development: Investigating an Integrated Framework". In *Disaster and Development: Examining Global Issues and Cases,* eds. N. Kapucu and K.T. Liou. Switzerland: Springer International Publishing. p. 3.

Mahajan, S. K., and A. Mahajan. 2015. "Politico-Administrative Response to the Impact of Hydropower on Nature and People: A Case Study". In *Strategic Disaster Risk Management in Asia,* eds. H. Ha, R. Lalitha, S. Fernando, and A. Mahmood. New Delhi: Springer, pp. 29–38.

Ministry of Home Affairs. 2018. "India Advocated Greater Investment in Improving Disaster Resilience for Recurrent Hazards." Retrieved from: http://pib.nic.in/newsite/PrintRelease.aspx?relid=180424

Mittal, R. 2017. *Kashmir and Me: A True Tale of Surviving a Flood.* New Delhi: Partridge Publishing.

Narain, S. 2016. "Why Urban India Floods, Indian Cities Grow at the Cost of their Wetlands". New Delhi: Centre for Science and Environment.

Narayan, P. 2018. "Displacement as Disaster Relief: Environmental gentrication and state informality in developing Chennai". In *Just Green Enough: Urban Development and Environmental Gentrification,* eds. W. Curran and T. Hamilton. London: Routledge.

National Disaster Management Authority. 2018. "Union Home Minister to Inaugurate IWDRI 2018". http://ndma.gov.in/images/pdf/pr-12jan.pdf

National Disaster Management Authority. 2009. *National Policy on Disaster Management. https://ndma.gov.in/images/guidelines/national-dm-policy2009.pdf*

National Disaster Management Authority Ministry of Home Affairs Government of India. 2016. *National Disaster Management Plan.* (NDMP). National Disaster Management Authority Ministry of Home Affairs Government of India https://ndma.gov.in/images/policyplan/dmplan/National%20Disaster%20Management%20Plan%20May%202016.pdf

Press Information Bureau. 2016. "Prime Minister's Address at Asian Ministerial Conference on Disaster Risk Reduction." http://pib.nic.in/newsite/PrintRelease.aspx?relid=153213

Rajya Sabha Secretariat. 2014. "Rescue, Rehabilitation and Reconstruction in the Aftermath of the Floods and Landslides in Jammu & Kashmir". New Delhi: Rajya Sabha Secretariat.

Rajya Sabha Secretariat. 2016. "Disaster in Chennai Caused by Torrential Rainfall and Consequent Flooding". New Delhi: Rajya Sabha Secretariat.

Samuel, M., P. Annadurai, and S. Sankarakrishnan. 2018. "The 2015 Chennai Floods, Green Social Work, An Emerging Model for Practice in India". In *The Routledge Handbook of Green Social Work* (pp. 281–292), eds. L. Dominelli. London and New York: Routledge.

Sharma, V. 2013. "The Role of Government and the Private Sector in Mitigating and Adapting to Climate Change". In *Governance Approaches to Mitigation of and Adaptation to Climate Change in Asia,* eds. H. Ha and T.N. Dhakal, 148-159. London, UK: Palgrave Macmillan.

Sharma, V., R. Agrawal, and K. Bharti. 2015. "Lack of Integrity Moving the Goals Away". In *Land and Disaster Management Strategies in Asia,* ed. H Ha, 139-153. New Delhi: Springer.

The Indian Express. December 8, 2015. "Chennai Floods: Industries crippled, Suffer Huge Revenue Loss". http://indianexpress.com/article/india/india-news-india/chennai-floods-industries-crippled-suffer-huge-revenue-loss

Uitto, J.I., and R. Shaw, eds. 2016. *Sustainable Development and Disaster Risk Reduction.* Japan: Springer.

United Nations. 2015. "Sendai Framework for Disaster Risk Reduction 2015-30". New York: United Nations.

Venugopal, R., and S. Yasir. 2017. "The Politics of Natural Disasters in Protracted Conflict: The 2014 Flood in Kashmir". *Oxford Development Studies* 45, no. 4, pp. 424–42.

CHAPTER 9

Disaster Risk Management in the Agricultural Sector in South Asia: Lessons Learned and Policy Implications

R. Lalitha S. Fernando

Department of Public Administration, University of Sri Jayewardenepura, Sri Lanka

Huong Ha

School of Business, Singapore University of Social Sciences, Singapore

Sanjeev Kumar Mahajan

Himachal Pradesh University, Shimla, India

Introduction

This book consists of nine chapters including the introduction and the conclusion, focusing mainly on disasters and its impacts on agriculture and how countries can become sustainable in terms of agriculture despite disasters. Excluding the introduction and concluding chapters, all other chapters are mainly based on case studies. A recap of the chapters is presented here. The first chapter provided a summary of each chapter. Chapter 2 by Namrata Agrawal and Disha Gupta examined the impact of natural disasters on humans and agriculture, which highlighted the existing disaster vulnerability in India. Chapter 3 by Rajesh Kumar analyzed India's preparedness and capabilities of handling nuclear disasters and mitigating the risks and moving toward being a disaster-resilience society. Chapter 4 by Fernando et al. identified the strengths and the weaknesses of the existing agriculture policy of Sri Lanka and proposed the best strategies to cope with disasters. Chapter 5 by Nasim Banu aimed to identify the impact of natural disasters on agricultural production in Bangladesh and examined selected activities that have been taking place in the public sector to minimize the agricultural loss and damage from natural disasters. Chapter 6 by Sanjeev Kumar Mahajan and Anupama Puri Mahajan analyzed India's preparedness and capabilities of handling nuclear disasters and mitigating the risks and moving toward being a disaster-resilience society. It discussed different dimensions of disaster risks in Himachal Pradesh in India and examined the impact of disasters due to monsoons over the years on the agricultural sector. Chapter 7 by Rabindranath Bhattacharyya and Jebunnessa examined the sustainability of the network of the public distribution system (PDS) of food grains in West Bengal and Bangladesh and recommended practical policies and guidelines in making the PDS more effective in a postdisaster situation. Chapter 8 by Himanshu Shekhar Mishra attempted to assess the impact of natural disasters on sustainable development processes in India.

Lessons Learned, Policy Implications, and Recommendations

Several common lessons are drawn from these chapters. As natural disasters are frequent occurrences, when observing rising trends of natural disasters, disaster risk management needs to be adopted as a multidimensional endeavor, including the use of ICT (information communication technology). Relevant authorities have to take realistic and informed policy decisions and plans with more investment in disaster risk management.

Nuclear power has potential to ensure long-term energy security. However, when implementing nuclear power programs, developing countries like India need to adopt a cautious path in the light of its needs as well as its realistic capability of managing nuclear disasters (Farrell 2018). Although, nuclear energy must be ingrained in the future energy policy-making, there is risk associated with nuclear power. Awareness programs for all citizens, including school education, need to be implemented with the aim of developing a new culture of resilience toward such disasters.

Natural disasters always create negative impact on agriculture, which in turn often places a lot of pressure on natural resources and the environment (Food and Agriculture Organization of the United Nations 2018, 2013). If the economy of a country largely depends on agriculture, then it is compulsory to promote sustainable agricultural practices to protect the environment. Implementation of sustainable agricultural policy should be marked as an urgent agenda item to ensure the survival patterns of rural farmers in Sri Lanka as their income level is lower because of the effect of disasters causing declines in crop yields. As natural disasters are major threats to sustainable agricultural production and its growth, a developing country like Bangladesh needs regional cooperation especially on water management initiatives to reduce the impact of disasters (Ha and Akbaruddin 2014). Neighboring countries need to work together to maintain regional cooperation for climate change management and protect and enhance citizen's collective common interests (Ha 2017; Ha, Fernando and Mahmood 2015a, b).

Overall, effective disaster risk reduction and management systems have to be systematically implemented in the agricultural sector. For example, crop insurance should be made compulsory to provide compensation and incentive to avoid losses arising out of disaster (Ozaki 2016). Warning systems should be initiated in cities/towns and villages, monitoring systems should be utilized to protect lives and properties, and an awareness campaign about the utility of the warning systems should be carried out extensively. Private sector contribution, citizen participation, and involvement of local-level authorities are also helpful in dealing with risk reduction (Ha 2017).

Also, reforms have to be implemented to ensure food security during the postdisaster situation. In this regard, comprehensive data systems containing various important data such as loss of workdays, damage to crops and crop area, impact on livelihood, insurance, relief and compensation amount, and immigration after disasters have to be maintained. Laws have to be strengthened to ensure the benefits for the disaster-affected people (e.g., *National Food Security Act* in Sri Lanka).

Limitations

This volume primarily focuses on disaster risk reduction toward sustainable agriculture with reference to India, Bangladesh, and Sri Lanka. However, there is no discussion related to other South Asian countries, such as Nepal and Pakistan. Furthermore, most of the writings are based on secondary sources with qualitative research methods. Thus, future work in the field could be undertaken relevant to other South Asian countries and with empirical data, and also with the use of a deductive approach.

Conclusion

The main focus of this volume is to discuss and analyze disaster risk reduction in the agriculture sector in relation to South Asia. The agriculture sector is the main economic backbone of the most developing countries including India, Bangladesh, and Sri Lanka. The agriculture sector has become more vulnerable because of the frequent occurrence of disasters. One of the most direct ways in which natural disasters affect the sector is through reduced production, and these results in direct economic loss to farmers, which can cascade along the entire value chain, affecting agricultural growth and rural livelihoods (Food and Agriculture Organization of the United Nations 2017). Effective strategies through administrative reforms are essential to cope with disaster to make agriculture more sustainable. To have effective strategies, sustainable management of natural resources and progressive enhancement of soil quality, biodiversity and productivity, and also several farming systems that can help produce more from the available land, water, and labor resources *without* either ecological or social harm to trigger the evergreen revolution have been identified (Kesavan and Swaminathan 2017).

In addressing disaster management, data collection, communication, cooperation, coordination, and raising public awareness are vital. Hence, effective information management is a vital process in this regard. Effective information management issues, such as reaching a defined addressee and being comprehensible, multisource, relevant, on time, reliable, and standardized have to be addressed (Wattegama 2007). Thus, the usage of ICT in the process of disaster risk reduction will lead to a sustainable agriculture system.

References

Farrell, J. 2018. "Fukushima nuclear disaster: Lethal levels of radiation detected in leak seven years after plant meltdown in Japan." *The Independent.* https://www.independent.co.uk/news/world/asia/fukushima-nuclear-disaster-radiation-lethal-levels-leak-japan-tsunami-tokyo-electric-power-company-a8190981.html

Food and Agriculture Organization of the United Nations. 2013. *FAO Annual Report 2013*. Rome, Italy: Food and Agriculture Organization of the United Nations. Food and Agriculture Organization of the United Nations. 2017. *The Impact of Disasters on Agriculture Addressing the Information Gap*. Rome, Italy: Food and Agriculture Organization of the United Nations.

Food and Agriculture Organization of the United Nations. 2018. *2017 The Impact of Disasters and Crises on Agriculture and Food Security*. Rome, Italy: Food and Agriculture Organization of the United Nations.

Ha, H. 2017. "Risk Governance and Disaster Impacts in Asia." Prevention Web, UN Office for Disaster Risk Reduction. http://www.preventionweb.net/experts/oped/view/55397

Ha, H., and A. Akbaruddin. 2014. "Bangladesh: Natural Disaster Risk Management." In *Land and Disaster Management Strategies in Asia*, ed. H. Ha. Germany/New Delhi: Springer, pp. 83–98.

Ha, H., L. Fernando, and A. Mahmood. 2015a. "Disaster Management in Asia: Lessons Learned and Policy Implications." In *Strategic Disaster Risk Management in Asia*, eds. H. Ha, L. Fernando, and A. Mahmood. Germany/New Delhi: Springer, pp. 221–6.

Ha, H., L. Fernando, and A. Mahmood. 2015b. "Strategic Disaster Risk Management in Asia: An Introduction." In *Strategic Disaster Risk Management in Asia*, eds. H. Ha, L. Fernando, and A. Mahmood. Germany/New Delhi: Springer, pp. 1–13.

Kesavan, P.C., and M.S. Swaminathan. 2017. "Strategies and Models for Agricultural Sustainability in Developing Asian Countries." *Journal of Philosophical Transaction B* 363, no. 1492, pp. 877–91.

Ozaki, M. 2016. "Disaster Risk Financing in Bangladesh, ADB South Asia." Working Paper Series, No. 46. Manila: Asian Development Bank.

Wattegama, C. 2007. *ICT for Disaster Management*. Bangkok: UNDP Regional Centre in Bangkok.

List of Contributors[1]

Professor Dr. **Namrata Agrawal** has more than 28 years of teaching, research, and consultancy experience. She has published more than 30 research papers in refereed national and international journals listed/indexed in SCI, SCOPUS, EBSCO, IEEE, Springer, US Cabell's Directory, Ulrich's Periodicals Directory, ERA, and Google Scholar. She has also presented around 40 papers in national and international conferences. She is the author of the following three books: (i) Comdex "Securing IT Infrastructure—A Complete Solution" authored by the undersigned, published under Wiley Dreamtech publisher. Kindle edition is also available. The book received a 5 star rating at amazon. in (highest rating at Amazon), (ii) "Cyber Security: Proceedings of CSI 2015 (Advances in Intelligent Systems and Computing)," jointly edited by Prof. M. U. Bokhari, professor, Aligarh Muslim University, Aligarh; Dr. Namrata Agrawal, professor, NIFM; and Dr. D. S. Saini, BVCOE, India, published by Springer in June 2018. The book may prove to be a useful source of reference for future researchers in the domain of cyber security, and (iii) New Comdex Tally, endorsed by Tally and authored by the undersigned, published under Wiley Dreamtech publisher. Kindle Edition is also available. The book received a 3½ star rating at amazon.in.

She has also guided several PhD students. She has vast international exposure and has traveled extensively to the United States, United Kingdom (London, Manchester), Scotland, Europe, Singapore, Malaysia, Philippines, Nepal, Bhutan, and Sri Lanka. She has successfully participated in the International Internship Certificate Program on "Budgeting, Accounting and Financial Management" of the "Edinburgh Business School," Scotland, in the year 2011. Her membership of professional bodies includes (i) member of Advisory Board of "The Modern Technology & Management Institute," USA, (ii) a life member of the Computer Society of India, and (iii) a life member of International body—Network

---

[1]The contributors' names are arranged according to the order of the chapters.

of Asia-Pacific Schools and Institutes of Public Administration and Governance initially supported by the Asian Development Bank and INTAN—Malaysia.

Disha Gupta is pursuing master of technology (cyber security and incident response) from Gujarat Forensic Sciences University (GFSU), India.

Rajesh Kumar is assistant professor of political science at the School of Social Sciences, Guru Nanak Dev University, Amritsar, Punjab, India. He has a doctoral degree from Jawaharlal Nehru University, New Delhi. Dr. Kumar's teaching and research interests are in areas of international relations, South Asian government and politics, foreign and security affairs. His publications include the book *Indo-U.S. Political and Strategic Relations* besides several articles contributed in journals like *Pakistan Horizon*, *World Focus*, *South Asian Affairs*, and *Punjab Journal of Politics*. He has contributed many chapters in edited volumes of national as well as international repute. He is alumni of the Summer Workshop, Regional Centre for Strategic Studies, Colombo, Sri Lanka. He is also member of Network of Asia-Pacific Schools and Institutes of Public Administration and Governance (NAPSIPAG), J.N.U., New Delhi, and several other professional bodies. He can be accessed at rkumargndu@gmail.com. His contact number is +91-9815949829.

Ms. **M.S. Dimuthu Kumari** serves as a lecturer in the Department of Public Administration, Faculty of Management Studies and Commerce, University of Sri Jayewardenepura, Sri Lanka. She is a young researcher and is interested in researching about disaster management and social issues.

Mr. **W.M.D.M. Dissanayaka** serves as a lecturer in the Department of Public Administration, Faculty of Management Studies and Commerce, University of Sri Jayewardenepura, Sri Lanka. He is a young researcher and is interested in researching on issues prevailing in the public sector and the environment.

Nasim Banu is a doctorate of social sciences who did her master's in public administration and MPhil in regional planning. She is a professor and present chairman, Department of Development Studies in Islamic University, Kushtia, Bangladesh. She has been teaching for the last 28 years and has published about 30 articles in reputed journals.

Public policy and disaster management is the field of her research area. Prof. Banu works closely with the policymakers and concerned agencies of Bangladesh in collecting information. She has attended a number of international conferences with her research works that aimed to monitor and evaluate the national policies and their impacts in transforming nationalization to privatization and poverty issues; to revisit the management practices and the participation of the international community in facing disasters in Bangladesh; to assess the suitability of plans, planning and nature of public financing of Bangladesh to address the impact of climate change.

Anupama Puri Mahajan, PhD, a researcher and a freelance writer, served as postdoctoral research fellow in the Department of Public Administration, Himachal Pradesh University, Shimla, India. She regularly contributes research articles to reputed journals of public administration, newspapers, and chapters in reputed books. She has authored and coauthored books on women empowerment and financial administration in India. Her two books on public administration and development administration are scheduled to be released before the end of the year 2018.

Dr. Rabindranath Bhattacharyya is currently the professor of political science in the University of Burdwan, West Bengal, India, where he has been teaching for more than 30 years. His research area focuses on disaster management and governance with special focus on poverty alleviation programs across countries and the role of government as well as different groups in that regard. He was appointed as an Australia Awards Ambassador by the Australian High Commissioner to India on March 28, 2014 for the year 2014 to 2015. He was awarded Australian Government Endeavour Post-Doctoral Research Award, 2009 at the UniSA and AIC Australian Studies (Senior) Visiting Fellowship 2007 to 2008 for visiting Curtin University, Perth; Hawke Research Institute, UniSA; RSPAS, Australian National University; Monas University, Melbourne; and School of History and Philosophy, UNSW, Sydney, in Australia. He has coedited three books: *Land, Leadership and Local Resource Management, Governance and Poverty Reduction—Beyond the Cage of Best Practices*, and *Essays on International Terrorism*. He has a number of papers and book chapters published in both national and international journals and books. He has presented papers and chaired sessions in various national and international conferences/seminars spread over eight countries other than India. He has successfully supervised PhD theses of five candidates from India and Bangladesh.

Dr. Jebunnessa is currently an associate professor (since 2003) and the chairperson of the Department of Public Administration, Jahangirnagar University. She obtained BSS Honors and MSS in Public Administration from the University of Dhaka, Bangladesh with First Class in 2000 and 2002, respectively. After that she joined as a Gender Training Officer of the Capacity Building for Gender Mainstreaming Project of UNDP. She taught at Gono Biswabidyalya (Private University) from 2006 to 2009. She was an assistant director of Bangladesh Energy Regulatory Commission for one year, which she left to join the post of lecturer in the Department of Public Administration at Jahangirnagar University in April 2010. In 2009, she earned M Phil in Public Administration from the Dhaka University. She earned PhD degree in 2017 from the Department of Political Science, the University of Burdwan, West Bengal, India. Her areas of research specialization are corruption, energy and regulatory governance, e-governance, public sector management and reform, women and gender, urban management and liberation war of Bangladesh. She has published a number of articles and books both in English and in Bengali in the research areas. She has also presented papers in different national and international seminars and conferences. She is also a member of a number of national and international professional and cultural associations.

Himanshu Shekhar Mishra works as editor (Government Affairs) in New Delhi Television. He was part of the Prime Minister's official entourage to the UN Annual Summit in New York (2003) and Indo-Turkish Summit in Ankara and Istanbul (2003). As a TV news correspondent, he has extensively reported on Indian politics and researched on disaster management. He has presented research papers at the 3rd UN World Conference on Disaster Risk Reduction (Sendai 2015), ASEAN University Network conferences in Manila (2015) and Kuala Lumpur (2016), Fudan University in Shanghai, IIT Roorkee, Jawaharlal Nehru University, and the World Congress on Disaster Management. His paper titled "Interrogating Right to Compensation in Disaster Laws: A Case Study of Kashmir Floods" was published in an edited volume titled "Disaster Laws, Emerging Thresholds" by Routledge in July 2017.

About the Authors

Dr. Huong Ha is head, Business Programme at School of Business, Singapore University of Social Sciences. She has been affiliated with the University of Newcastle, Australia. Her previous positions include dean, director of research and development, deputy course director, chief editor, executive director, business development manager, and so forth. She holds a PhD from Monash University (Australia) and a master's degree from National University of Singapore. She was a recipient of a PhD scholarship (Monash University), Temasek scholarship (National University of Singapore), and a scholarship awarded by the United Nations University/International Leadership Academy, and many other scholarships, professional and academic awards, and research-related grants. She has authored or co-edited the following books: *Climate Change: Special Topics in the Context of Asia (BEP)*, *Change Management for Sustainability (BEP)*, *Land and Disaster Management Strategies in Asia (Springer)*, *Governance Approaches to Mitigation of and Adaptation to Climate Change in Asia (Palgrave Macmillan)*, and *Strategic Disaster Risk Management in Asia (Springer)*. She has also produced about 80 journal articles, book chapters, conference papers, and articles in encyclopedias. She has been an invited member of the international editorial boards of many international journals/book projects in many countries; the scientific and/or technical committees of several international conferences in many countries; and international advisory boards of many associations. She has also been a reviewer of many international journals and international conferences.

Professor (Dr.) R. Lalitha S. Fernando serves as a senior professor in the Department of Public Administration and as the director of research, Centre of Governance and Public Policy of the University of Sri Jayewardenepura in Sri Lanka. Currently, she is the secretary general of the Network of Asia-Pacific Schools and Institutes of Public Administration and Governance. She was awarded the prestigious Commonwealth

Academic (internal) Scholarship and the master's degree in development administration and management by the University of Manchester, United Kingdom. In addition, she was awarded a full-time scholarship to pursue her PhD at Graduate School of Public Administration, National Institute of Development Administration (NIDA), Thailand. She has published a number of papers, book chapters, conference papers, and articles and has coedited books related to public management, governance, and environmental management and educational management at both national and international levels.

Sanjeev Kumar Mahajan, PhD, professor of public administration and dean, Faculty of Social Sciences, Himachal Pradesh University, Shimla (India), has had a brilliant academic career. He was awarded the university medal for standing first in the MA and MPhil programs by the Panjab University, Chandigarh. He has presented research articles at several national and international conferences. He has authored and coedited books on public sector, public administration, governance, and financial administration in India. In addition, he holds many important administrative positions in the university. His areas of specialization include public enterprises, transport management, financial administration, and disaster-related issues.

Index

OTHER TITLES FROM THE ECONOMICS AND PUBLIC POLICY COLLECTION

Philip Romero, The University of Oregon and
Jeffrey Edwards, North Carolina A&T State University, *Editors*

- *A Primer on Microeconomics, Second Edition, Volume II: Competition and Constraints* by Thomas M. Beveridge
- *A Primer on Microeconomics, Second Edition, Volume I: Fundamentals of Exchange* by Thomas M. Beveridge
- *A Primer on Macroeconomics, Second Edition, Volume II: Policies and Perspectives* by Thomas M. Beveridge
- *A Primer on Macroeconomics, Second Edition, Volume I: Elements and Principles* by Thomas M. Beveridge
- *Macroeconomics, Second Edition, Volume I* by David G. Tuerck
- *Macroeconomics, Second Edition, Volume II* by David G. Tuerck
- *Economic Renaissance In the Age of Artificial Intelligence* by Apek Mulay
- *Disaster Risk Management: Case Studies in South Asian Countries* by Huong Ha, R. Lalitha S. Fernando, and Sanjeev Kumar Mahajan
- *The Option Strategy Desk Reference: An Essential Reference for Option Traders* by Russell A. Stultz

Announcing the Business Expert Press Digital Library

Concise e-books business students need for classroom and research

This book can also be purchased in an e-book collection by your library as

- *a one-time purchase,*
- *that is owned forever,*
- *allows for simultaneous readers,*
- *has no restrictions on printing, and*
- *can be downloaded as PDFs from within the library community.*

Our digital library collections are a great solution to beat the rising cost of textbooks. E-books can be loaded into their course management systems or onto students' e-book readers. The **Business Expert Press** digital libraries are very affordable, with no obligation to buy in future years. For more information, please visit **www.businessexpertpress.com/librarians**. To set up a trial in the United States, please email **sales@businessexpertpress.com**.

www.ingramcontent.com/pod-product-compliance
Lightning Source LLC
Chambersburg PA
CBHW061307220326
41599CB00026B/4770